Internet Research

ILLUSTRATED, THIRD EDITION

Donald I. Barker
Carol D. Terry

THOMSON

COURSE TECHNOLOGY ™

Australia • Canada • Mexico • Singapore • Spain • United Kingdom • United States

Internet Research—Illustrated, Third Edition

Donald I. Barker, Carol D. Terry

Executive Editor: Rachel Goldberg	**Developmental Editor:** MT Cozzola	**Text Designer:** Joseph Lee, Black Fish Design
Senior Acquisitions Editor: Marjorie Hunt	**Production Editor:** Jill Klaffky	**Copy Editor/Proofreader:** Karen Annett
Senior Product Manager: Christina Kling Garrett	**Senior Marketing Manager:** Joy Stark-Vancs	**Composition House:** GEX Publishing Services
Associate Product Manager: Shana Rosenthal	**Marketing Coordinator:** Melissa Marcoux	**Indexer:** Rich Carlson
Editorial Assistant: Janine Tangney	**QA Manuscript Reviewers:** Jeff Schwartz, Ashlee Welz, Susan Whalen	

The Illustrated Series Vision

Teaching and writing about computer applications and information literacy can be extremely challenging but rewarding. How do we engage students and keep their interest? How do we teach them skills that they can easily apply on the job? As we set out to write this book, our goals were to develop a textbook that:

- works for a beginning student

- provides varied, flexible, and meaningful exercises and projects to reinforce the skills

- serves as a reference tool

- makes your job as an educator easier, by providing a variety of supplementary resources to help you teach your course

Our popular, streamlined format is based on feedback we've received over the years from instructional designers and customers. This flexible design presents each lesson on a two-page spread, with step-by-step instructions on the left, and screen illustrations on the right. This signature style, coupled with high-caliber content, provides a comprehensive introduction to the crucial skills of conducting Internet research and a rich learning experience for the student.

Author Acknowledgments

Creating a book is a team effort. We would like to thank: our spouses, Chia-Ling Barker and Paul Turner, for their unfailing patience and generous support; Marjorie Hunt for publishing the book; Christina Kling Garrett for managing the project; and our excellent developmental editor, MT Cozzola, for corrections and invaluable suggestions.
Donald I. Barker and Carol D. Terry

Preface

Welcome to *Internet Research—Illustrated, Third Edition*. Each lesson in the book contains elements pictured to the right in the sample two-page spread.

How is the book organized?

The book is organized into four units on conducting effective Internet research, from conducting basic searches with search engines using keywords and phrases, to creating complex searches using Boolean logic. Subject guides and specialized tools are also covered, including periodical databases, government resources, online reference sources, mailing lists, newsgroups, and intelligent search agents.

What kinds of assignments are included in the book? At what level of difficulty?

The lesson assignments use the interesting and relevant case study of alternative energy. As part of the city planning office in Portland, Oregon, you conduct research on different energy resources that will help the city to become "energy independent." The assignments are found on the light purple pages at the end of each unit and they progressively increase in difficulty. Assignments include:

- **Concepts Reviews** to test your knowledge with multiple choice, matching, and screen identification questions.

- **Skills Reviews** to provide additional hands-on, step-by-step reinforcement.

- **Independent Challenges** that are case projects requiring critical thinking and application of the skills learned in the unit. The Independent Challenges increase in difficulty, with the first Independent Challenge in each unit being the easiest (with the most step-by-step, detailed instructions).

Each 2-page spread focuses on a single skill.

Concise text that introduces the basic principles in the lesson and integrates the brief case study (indicated by the paintbrush icon).

UNIT B
Internet Research

Searching with Filters

Another way to refine a search is to use filters. **Filters** are programs that tell search tools to screen out specified types of Web pages or files. They are usually located on advanced search pages. As you develop your search strategy, use filters to search only a specified area of the Web or to exclude specified areas of the Web. For example, you use language filters to search only for pages in English, or date filters to search only for pages updated in the last year, or for certain file types such as images, audio, or video. Table B-5 lists examples of filter options available on Google's Advanced Search page. One of your team members read that Denmark is a leader in wind power. You want to see some Danish sites, but because you don't read Danish, you need to find pages that are in English. Bob suggests you use filters on an advanced search page to focus the search. He tells you that the domain for Denmark is .dk.

STEPS

QUICK TIP
For more complex Boolean searches, it is usually more efficient to use the Basic Search page. This reduces the chances of inadvertent logic errors.

QUICK TIP
The Domains filter lets you choose between "Only return results from the site or domain" or "*Don't return results from the site or domain.*" In this search, you want it to read *Only*.

1. **At the Google site, click** Advanced Search, **then click your browser's** Refresh button **to clear the text boxes if necessary**
   The Google Advanced Search page includes a number of convenient options to simplify constructing Boolean searches involving only a few keywords or phrases.

2. **Click the** Language list box, **then click** English
   See Figure B-11. With this filter, your search results will only include Web pages written in English. Now you want to restrict your search to the domain exclusive to Denmark.

3. **Type** .dk **in the Domain text box**
   See Figure B-11. With this filter, your search results will only include Web pages from Denmark.

4. **Type** wind power **in the with the exact phrase text box, then click** Search
   Quotation marks are not needed to indicate a phrase search. This specialized text box interprets any words typed here as a phrase, so quotation marks are assumed. Figure B-12 illustrates the results in a Venn diagram. The Web pages returned contain the phrase *wind power*, are in English, and are from Denmark's domain.

5. **Use the** Searching with Filters table **in your document to record the number of search results, then save your document**
   Note that Google has translated your search as "*wind power*" site:.dk. Quotation marks show how Google interpreted the words you typed into the "with the exact phrase" box. The site:.dk is how Google translated your domain filter selection. Just below the tabs you see that Google searched only pages in English. Google reiterates your query as Searched *English* pages for "*wind power*" site:.dk. Check this information to determine if the filters worked the way you expected when you developed the search strategy.

TABLE B-5: Commonly used filters on Google's Advanced Search page

Language	Limits search to pages written in the language you choose (English, French, Japanese, etc.)
File Format	Limits search to pages in the format you choose (.pdf, .xls, .doc, etc.)
Date	Limits search to pages updated within a specified time period (3, 6, or 12 months)
Occurrences	Limits search to pages containing your keywords in the location you choose (URL, title, links, etc.)
Domain	Limits search to include pages only with a specified domain or to exclude pages with a specified domain
SafeSearch	Limits search by filtering to exclude potentially offensive pages (can be hit and miss)

34 UNIT B: CONSTRUCTING COMPLEX SEARCHES

Hints as well as troubleshooting advice, right where you need it—next to the step itself.

Quickly accessible summaries of key terms, toolbar buttons, or keyboard alternatives connected with the lesson material. Students can refer easily to this information when working on their own projects at a later time.

Every lesson features large, full-color representations of what the screen should look like as students complete the numbered steps.

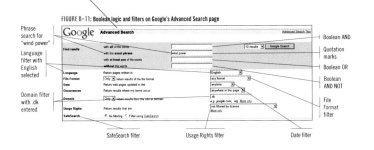

FIGURE B-11: Boolean logic and filters on Google's Advanced Search page

Phrase search for "wind power"

Language filter with English selected

Domain filter with .dk entered

Boolean AND

Quotation marks

Boolean OR

Boolean AND NOT

File Format filter

SafeSearch filter   Usage Rights filter   Date filter

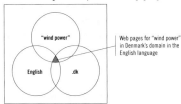

FIGURE B-12: Venn diagram for: "wind power" domain:.dk language: English

"wind power"

English   .dk

Web pages for "wind power" in Denmark's domain in the English language

Clues to Use

Filtering domains in the URL

Filters search only for letters or words that appear in certain parts of a URL. The final two or three letters in the URL indicate domains. Web sites in the United States have URLs that end in three letters that represent the type of organization hosting the Web site. For example: university sites end in .edu; government sites end in .gov; commercial sites end in .com; and nonprofits end in .org. Others include: .biz, .pro, .info, .net, .us, .coop, .museum, and .name. Web sites located in other countries use two-letter country codes: Canada's domain is .ca; the United Kingdom's domain is .uk; Japan's domain is .jp. Any of these two- or three-letter codes can limit search results when using a domain filter. For a full listing of the two-letter country codes, go to www.iana.org/cctld/cctld-whois.htm. You can find other sites with this information by searching for *countries* AND *domains*.

Internet Research

Clues to Use boxes provide concise information that either expands on the major lesson skill or describes an independent task that in some way relates to the major lesson skill.

Subsequent Independent Challenges become increasingly open-ended, requiring more independent thinking and problem solving.

• **Advanced Challenge Exercises** set within the Independent Challenges provide optional tasks for more advanced students.

• **Visual Workshops** are practical, self-graded capstone projects that require independent problem solving.

What Web resources supplement the book?

Internet Research–Illustrated, Third Edition features an Online Companion Web site www.course.com/illustrated/research3. Use the Online Companion to access all the links referenced in the book, and to access other resources for further information. Since the Internet and search engines change frequently, the Online Companion will also contain any updates or clarifications to the text after its publication.

Instructor Resources

The Instructor Resources CD puts the resources and information needed to teach and learn effectively directly into your hands. This integrated array of teaching and learning tools offers you and your students a broad range of technology-based instructional options, and we believe this CD represents the highest quality, most cutting edge resources available to instructors today. Many of the components are available at www.course.com. The resources available with this book are:

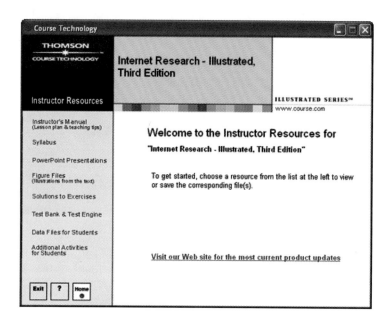

Instructor's Manual-Available as an electronic file, the Instructor's Manual is quality-assurance tested and includes unit overviews and detailed lecture topics with teaching tips for each unit.

Sample Syllabus-Prepare and customize our course easily using this sample course outline.

PowerPoint Presentations-Each unit has a corresponding PowerPoint Presentation that you can use in lecture, distribute to your students, or customize to suit your course.

Figure Files-The figures in the text are provided on the Instructor Resources CD to help you illustrate key topics or concepts. You can create traditional overhead transparencies by printing the figure files. Or you can create electronic slide shows by using the figures in a presentation program such as PowerPoint.

Solutions to Exercises-Solutions to Exercises contain every file students are asked to create or modify in the lessons and End-of-Unit material. A Help file on the Instructor Resources CD includes information for

using the Solution Files. There is also a document outlining the solutions for the End-of-Unit Concepts Review, Skills Review, and Independent Challenges.

ExamView Test Bank and Test Engine-ExamView is a powerful testing software package that allows you to create and administer printer, computer (LAN-based), and Internet exams. ExamView includes hundreds of questions that correspond to the topics covered in this text, enabling students to generate detailed study guides that include page references for further review. The computer-based and Internet testing components allow students to take exams at their computers, and also saves you time by grading each exam automatically.

Data Files for Students-To complete most of the units in this book, your students will need **Data Files**. Put them on a file server for students to copy. The Data Files are available on the Instructor Resources CD-ROM, the Review Pack, and can also be downloaded from www.course.com.

Brief Contents

Contents

Read This Before You Begin

Are there any prerequisites for this book?

This book focuses on using the Internet effectively as a powerful research tool. It assumes that you are familiar with the Internet and Internet terms, and know basic Web-browsing skills. Basic Web-browsing skills include using the menus and toolbars in the browser of your choice, entering URLs, and navigating the Web using hyperlinks. In order to complete the exercises using the Data Files, you should also have basic word-processing skills.

What software do I need in order to use this book?

You will need an Internet connection, a Web browser, and a text-editing or word-processing program such as Microsoft Word or WordPad, in order to complete the lessons and exercises in this book. You can be running any recent version of the Windows operating system after and including Windows 95, Linux, and the Mac operating systems. This book was written and tested using Microsoft Internet Explorer 6 and Microsoft Windows XP. If you are working with a different browser or in a different operating system, your screens might look slightly different from those shown in the book. Data Files have been verified in these environments.

What are Data Files and how do I use them?

Data Files are text files in Microsoft Word format that you use to answer questions about your research results. You use a Data File in most lessons and in some of the exercises. Typically, you open the designated file and save it with a new name.

What is the Online Companion and how do I use it?

You use the Online Companion, located at www.course.com/illustrated/research3, to access all the links used in the book. Because the Internet and its search engines change frequently, the Online Companion will provide updates to the text as necessary. To access the Online Companion quickly, add the URL to your Favorites or Bookmarks, or set it as your home page. (If you are working in a lab, ask your instructor before doing this.) The URL is provided throughout the book in steps and tips for easy reference as well.

Credits

Figures A-9, A-10: Microsoft product screen shot(s) reprinted with permission from Microsoft Corporation.
Figures A-7, A-8, A-12, A-13, A-14, A-15, A-19, B-3, B-5, B-7, B-11, B-13, B-14, D-15: GoogleTM is a trademark of Google Inc., (www.google.com).
Figures B-15, B-15: Courtesy of Ixquick, (www.ixquick.com).
Figure B-21: Courtesy of Quotationsbook.com.
Figures C-1, C-2, C-3, C-5: Courtesy of Librarians' Internet Index, (www.lii.org).
Figures C-4, C-6: Courtesy of The Open Directory Project, (www.dmoz.org).
Figures C-7, C-8: Courtesy of BUBL Information Service, (bubl.ac.uk).
Figures C-9, C-10, C-11, D-14: Courtesy of the U.S. Department of Energy, Energy Efficiency and Renewable Energy (www.eere.energy.gov).
Figures C-12, C-13, C-14: Courtesy of the Source for Renewable Energy, Momentum Technologies LLC, (energy.sourceguides.com).
Figure C-16: Courtesy of the Florida Solar Energy Center, Hydrogen Research and Applications Center, (www.fsec.ucf.edu).
Figures C-17, C-18: Courtesy of the Database of State Incentives for Renewable Energy (www.dsireusa.org).
Figure C-19: Courtesy of the University of California, Riverside, (infomine.ucr.edu).
Figure C-20: Courtesy of the National Health Information Center, U.S. Department of Health and Human Services, (www.healthfinder.gov).
Figure C-21: Courtesy of hockeydb.com.
Figures D-2, D-3, D-4: Reproduced with permission of Yahoo! Inc. YAHOO! and the YAHOO! logo are trademarks of Yahoo! Inc., (www.yahoo.com).
Figures D-5, D-6, D-7: ©2006 InfoSpace, Inc. All rights reserved. Reprinted with permission of InfoSpace, Inc.
Figures D-8, D-9: Courtesy of Hot Neuron LLC, (http://www.magportal.com/).
Figures D-10, D-11: Courtesy of the Federal citizen Information Center for FirstGov, (www.firstgov.gov). FirstGov.gov is the U.S. government's official Web portal to all federal, state, and local government Web resources and services.
Figures: D-13, D-14, D-15: Reproduced with permission of the Internet Public Library, Regents of the University of Michigan, (www.ipl.org).
Figures D-16, D-17, D-18: Courtesy of LOOP Improvements LLC, IncyWincy, (www.incywincy.com).
Figure D-19: Courtesy of Kazzoom, (www.kazzoom.com).

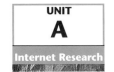
Searching the Internet Effectively

OBJECTIVES

Understand Internet search tools
Create an Internet research strategy
Identify the right keywords
Perform a basic search
Add keywords
Phrase search
Analyze search results
Cite online resources

The **World Wide Web** is an enormous repository of information stored on millions of computers all over the world. The **Internet** is a vast global network of interconnected networks that allows you to find and connect to information on the World Wide Web. Finding information on the Web is deceptively easy. In fact, finding lots of information is easier than finding the right information. In this unit, you will learn about types of Internet search tools, how to develop a search strategy to transform your initial question into an effective **search query**, how to perform basic searches, how to analyze your search results, and how to use a standardized format to cite Web pages. You work in the City Planning Office in Portland, Oregon. A proposition has recently passed that mandates the city work toward becoming energy independent in the near future. You are working with a team to create a list of useful Web resources. Your area of responsibility is to identify resources on the Web related to alternative energy. Although you have surfed the Web, you realize your skills need some polishing to do a quality job with this important assignment. You have a friend, Bob Johnson, who is a librarian at a Portland university library, and you ask him to help you learn the basics of Internet searching.

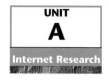

UNIT A

Internet Research

Understanding Internet Search Tools

Internet search tools are services that help you locate information on the Web and the Internet. Search tools can be divided into four major categories: search engines, metasearch engines, subject guides, and specialized search tools. Different search tools are better for finding different types of information, and no tool searches the entire Internet. Figure A-1 illustrates the four types of search tools and the main areas of the Internet and Web that these different search tools reach. ▰▰▰▰ Before you start your search for Web pages about alternative energy, Bob gives you a brief overview of the different search tools.

DETAILS

Types of search tools include the following:

> **QUICK TIP**
>
> To find out more about search engines, click the Search Engine Watch link or the Search Engine Showdown link on the Online Companion at www.course.com/ illustrated/research3.

- **Search engines** enable you to locate Web pages that contain keywords you enter in a search form. **Keywords** are the nouns and verbs, and sometimes important adjectives, that describe the major concepts of your search topic. A program called a **spider** crawls or scans the Web to index the keywords in Web pages. The indexes, or indices, created by spiders match the keywords you enter in a search engine and return a list of links to Web pages that contain these keywords. Because this is a precise process, it provides a narrow search of the Web and works well for finding specific content. Because spiders take months to index even a small portion of the Web, search engine results are limited and some might be out of date. No single search engine covers the entire Web, so consider using more than one engine for important searches.

- **Metasearch engines** offer a single search form to query multiple search engines simultaneously. As with search engines, you enter keywords to retrieve links to Web pages that contain matching information. Search results are compiled from other search engines, rather than from the Web. Metasearches are useful for quickly providing the highest ranked results from multiple search engines. Better metasearch engines remove duplicate results and rank the results based on relevancy to your query. Unfortunately, these results might not be optimal; the best search engines are often excluded from a metasearch because they charge fees, which metasearch engine providers decline to pay.

> **QUICK TIP**
>
> If you don't know much about the subject you need to research, a subject guide is often a good place to start online.

- **Subject guides** offer hierarchically organized topical directories that you navigate through to find relevant links. This design makes subject guides a good choice for a broad view of a topic. Subject guides are typically prepared by hand and vary in selectivity, criteria for inclusion, qualifications of human indexers, and levels of maintenance. Some are professional or academic sponsored, whereas others are commercial. Better subject guides also provide keyword searches of their database.

> **QUICK TIP**
>
> Major search engines constantly work toward being able to search parts of the Web that are currently invisible to their spiders.

- **Specialized search tools** allow you to find information that is "invisible" to traditional search engines or subject guides because it is stored in proprietary databases or in specialty directories, reference sites, and newsgroups. The vast majority of the information on the Web is in this invisible area, usually called the **deep Web**. To retrieve this information, you must go to a specific site and use its unique search interface. Although many of these sites require **subscriptions** or fees for access, some can be searched with a relatively newer breed of software, called **intelligent search agents**, which can query multiple specialty sites and/or search engines simultaneously. Intelligent search agents can actually search more of the Internet than conventional search tools such as search engines and subject guides.

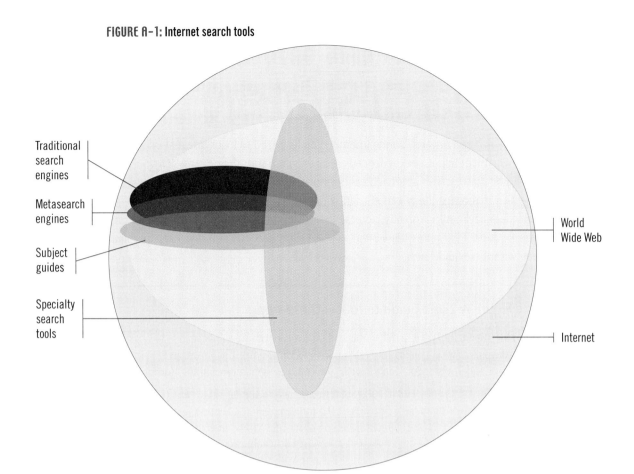

Parts of the Web searched by search engines and subject guides (blue, pink, and green) represent content in the visible or surface Web. Parts of the Web searched by specialty search tools (light blue), *and not* searched by search engines and subject guides, represent the invisible or deep Web. This conceptual graphic is not to scale and does not represent to what depth these tools actually penetrate the Internet and the Web; if it were to scale, the areas representing the unsearched Web and the Internet would be hundreds of times larger than they appear here.

Clues to Use

Using a search toolbar

Google, MSN, and Yahoo! provide search toolbars that enable you to search the Internet from your desktop, without actually visiting the search engines. Although each toolbar is closely tied to its parent search engine, they share many features in common, such as the ability to block pop-ups, automatically complete forms, and protect against Spyware. The Google Search Toolbar (http://toolbar. google.com/) checks the spelling of your queries, translates English words into other languages, and turns street addresses into links to online maps. The MSN Search Toolbar (http://toolbar.msn.com/) uses tabbed browsing to easily switch between Web pages and gives you one-click access to Hotmail, MSN Messenger, MSN Spaces, or My MSN. The Yahoo! Search Toolbar (http://companion. yahoo.com/) provides one-click access to features on its site, such as My Yahoo!, mail, and news. The Ixquick toolbar (http://us.ixquick.com/eng/aboutixquick/) provides quick metasearching and telephone directory searching, magnification buttons, and e-mail emoticons.

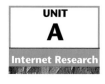

Creating an Internet Research Strategy

Before you begin a search on the Internet, you first need to focus on what information you want to find and how you might find it. Inexperienced searchers often start their online searching without giving thought to a plan or strategy. This approach can produce an overwhelming list of mostly useless results. However, an effective research strategy can efficiently produce more relevant, useful results. The following seven steps provide guidelines that greatly increase the likelihood of finding the information you need in a timely manner. Figure A-2 illustrates these steps. ░░░░ Bob suggests you develop a research strategy and provides you with these guidelines.

DETAILS

Use Figure A-2 as a guide to follow these steps:

- **Define your topic and note initial keywords**
  Ask yourself what you want to end up with when you finish your research. Write down your topic. Note keywords and phrases. You don't have to use complete sentences, but be thorough in identifying concepts.

QUICK TIP
If you get stuck at any point in your research, consult your local reference librarians. They are information experts.

- **Locate background information and identify additional keywords**
  If you initially know very little about the topic you are researching, look for general information in encyclopedias, periodicals, and reference sources first. They can give you a good foundation for your research and provide keywords to use in your search. When you come across potentially useful keywords, note them and their correct spellings so you can use them in your search query.

- **Choose the proper search tool**
  If the Web is a good place to look for your topic, you need to decide where to look. Use the search tools that are best suited to retrieving the type of information you want to find. Table A-1 lists the most common search tools and provides information on how to select the best tool for your research needs. If you want specific content, search engines or metasearch engines are appropriate. For a broader view, or when you know less about your topic, use subject guides. When seeking information not normally tracked by these tools, turn to specialty search tools. Combining these search tools provides the most thorough approach.

- **Translate your question into an effective search query**
  The first step in translating a question into an effective **search query**—which consists of a word, words, phrases, and symbols that a search engine can interpret—is to identify the keywords that best describe the topic. You use keywords to query either search engines or metasearch engines. You also use keywords to construct complex searches for even more accuracy.

- **Perform your search**
  Search engines offer a variety of different **search forms**, which contain fields in which you enter information specific to your search. Although some subject guides allow keyword searches, they are often searched by clicking through a series of links. In either case, the information you provide is used to return search results. Search results are the Web pages the search tool returns to you in response to your search query.

- **Evaluate your search results**
  The quantity and quality of results vary from one search engine to another. To ascertain the value of the information you find, you need to apply **evaluative criteria**, such as who authored the Web page or how current the information is.

- **Refine your search, if needed**
  You might need to go back to a previous step in the research process to refine your strategy if the quality or quantity of results is not what you need. Use what you learned from your first pass through this process to refine your search. First, try fine-tuning your search query, and then try a different search tool. If you are still not satisfied with your results, you might need to reevaluate your keywords. Perhaps they are too specific or obscure. If you are unable to do this or it isn't successful, you might need to seek more basic information on your topic. Or, rethink the topic—you might find that redefining it, based on what you have seen in your searches, would be helpful.

FIGURE A-2: Developing a research strategy

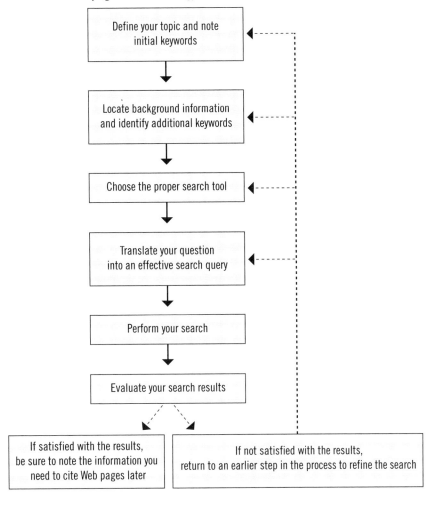

TABLE A-1: Common search tools

search tool	best for	where it searches	how to search	example information	example tools
Search engines	General or specific	Searches its own indexes that are compiled from data gathered from the Web	Enter keywords, phrases, or complex searches	Alternative energy or solar panels	Google AltaVista
Metasearch engines	General or specific	Searches the indexes of multiple search engines simultaneously	Enter keywords, phrases, or complex searches	Alternative energy or solar panels	Ixquick Vivisimo
Subject guides	More general	Searches its own files or database	Click through subject categories (may also allow keyword searches)	Alternative energy	Librarians' Internet Index WWW Virtual Library
Specialized tools	More specific	Searches databases, directories, reference sites, newsgroups, and search engines	Enter keywords, phrases, or complex searches	Latest news on solar panels	IncyWincy The Source for Renewable Energy

Internet Research

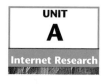

Identifying the Right Keywords

After you have identified your research topic, you need to translate it into a search strategy that optimizes your chances of finding useful information. The main elements in your search strategy are the keywords that describe the major concepts of your search topic. It is these keywords that you enter into the search tool and which the search tool uses to return results. Bob provides you with the following guidelines to help you create a list of keywords to use in your search for Web resources on alternative energy.

DETAILS

Follow these guidelines to create a list of keywords:

- **Write a sentence or two that summarizes your research topic**
  You want to find Web resources on alternative energy. The sentence shown in Figure A-3 demonstrates how to state your research topic.

- **Study the research topic and pull out potential keywords**
  You look at this topic and decide the words that could be used as keywords are *alternative* and *energy*. You circle these words, as shown in Figure A-4. By identifying these words, you are starting to turn your topic statement into terms that an Internet search tool can use effectively. Remember, these are the words you expect to appear on the Web pages that might be useful for your project. Search engines normally do not search for the words *a*, *an*, and *the*, so you should not include them in most searches. See Table A-2 for typical words that do not qualify as keywords, also known as **stop words**.

- **If necessary, define the keywords and find general background information on your topic**
  If you know very little about the topic you are researching, some initial research can help you identify useful keywords. You look in a dictionary and see that alternative energy is considered energy from nonfossil fuels. It mentions *solar* and *wind* as examples. You then look in an encyclopedia to read a bit more about alternative energy. You find other types of alternative energies that might be useful, including *water*, *biomass*, and *geothermal*. Figure A-5 illustrates how to list the keywords you identified for your research topic.

- **Identify synonyms and related terms for the keywords**
  Synonyms are words that have similar meanings. The meanings don't have to be exactly the same, just close. Useful Web pages have likely been created by many different people, using different words to describe the same topic. By expanding your list of keywords, you help ensure that your queries are broad enough to find Web pages not indexed under the exact keywords in your initial list. Figure A-6 demonstrates how to list your identified synonyms and related terms.

> **QUICK TIP**
> As you review search results, keep this list of keywords and synonyms handy. You might find new words that might be useful if you refine your search later. Also, the words can help you identify topics in the pages you find.

TABLE A-2: Common words that are not useful in most searches

parts of speech	examples
Articles	a, an, the
Conjunctions and prepositions	and, or, but, in, of, for, on, into, from, than, at, to
Adjectives and adverbs	as, also, probably, however, very
Pronouns and verbs	this, that, these, those, is, be, see, do

FIGURE A-3: Write down your research topic statement

I want to find Web resources on alternative energy

FIGURE A-4: Circle the keywords in your statement

I want to find Web resources on (alternative) (energy)

FIGURE A-5: Identify and list additional keywords

Keywords

alternative

energy

solar

wind

water

biomass

geothermal

FIGURE A-6: Identify synonyms and related words

Keywords	Synonyms & Related Terms
alternative	renewable, sustainable
energy	power
solar	panels, photovoltaic
wind	turbines, windmills
water	hydropower, hydroelectric
biomass	waste-to-energy, bioenergy
geothermal	heat, pumps

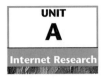

Performing a Basic Search

All search engines offer basic searching; however, they often differ in how they perform the search. It is always a good idea to view each search engine's Help page before you use it. An effective search statement at one search engine might not produce the best results at another. You can overcome these inconsistencies by using a trial-and-error approach to searching. At each search engine, try subtle variations on the search, changing your wording slightly. Note which search engines perform best for different kinds of searches. Over time, you will learn which search engines give you the best results for different subjects. You are ready to conduct a basic search using keywords you identified for alternative energy.

STEPS

TROUBLE

Web sites are constantly changing, so if you can't find the exact link or text box cited in the text, look for one with a similar name or purpose. If you need additional assistance, see your instructor.

QUICK TIP

Visit www.Search EngineWatch.com for information about which engines accept sponsored placement.

1. **Start your word-processing program, open the file IR A-1.doc from the drive and folder where your Data Files are located, then add your name at the top of the document**

   You can use this document to keep track of your search results. It is organized by lesson. You use the same document throughout the lessons in a unit, switching between the document and your browser as necessary.

2. **Click File on the menu bar, click Save As, navigate to the location where you are saving files for this book, create a new folder named *YourName* (your first and last name, without spaces,) then save the document as Searching the Internet in this new folder**

3. **Start your Web browser, go to the Online Companion at www.course.com/illustrated/ research3, then click the Google link (under "Search engines")**

   The Google search form opens, as shown in Figure A-7.

4. **Click in the Search text box, type solar energy, then click Search**

   Your results should look similar to Figure A-8. Be aware that many search engines accept payment for higher placement, so these sites, usually .com sites, are listed where you typically expect the best matching results. Better search engines indicate this, sometimes with the word "Sponsored." However, they are not required to disclose this.

5. **In the Performing a Basic Search table in your document, record how many results were found, delete your previous query in the Search text box, type solar power, then click Search**

   Notice that the browser displays a different number of results for this search than the last. One small change in a search query can radically change the number and quality of search results. Also, note that the number of results displayed often includes multiple pages per site; that is, a site with multiple pages on your topic might be returned more than once in your results.

6. **Record the number of results in the same table in your document**

   You know that using a different search tool can alter results, so you decide to try your search using AOL.

7. **Go to the Online Companion, then click the AOL Search link (under "Search engines")**

8. **Click in the Search text box, type solar energy, click search, then in the same table in your document, record the number of pages of results this search found**

QUICK TIP

Most search tools allow either pressing Enter or clicking Search to start a search.

9. **Delete your previous query in the Search text box, type solar power, press [Enter], record the number of pages this search found in the same table in your document, then save your document**

   Notice again that your browser displays a different number of results for this search than the last.

FIGURE A-7: Google search form

Links to kinds of searches (*Web search is the default selection*)

Search text box

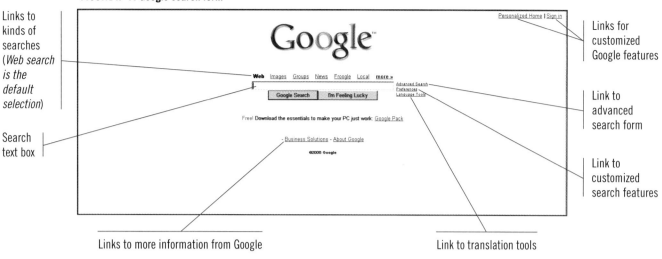

Links for customized Google features

Link to advanced search form

Link to customized search features

Links to more information from Google

Link to translation tools

FIGURE A-8: Google search for *solar energy*

Your search

Sponsored results

Links to results in recent news

Search results

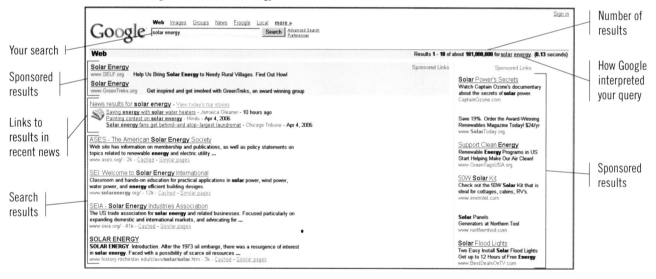

Number of results

How Google interpreted your query

Sponsored results

Clues to Use

Why do search results vary with different search engines?

When a search engine spider scans the Internet for Web pages, it finds only a fraction of the Web pages that exist for any given topic. Each engine's spiders crawl different parts of the Web and a different scope of content. So when you use a different search engine, you are actually searching a slightly different part and a slightly different range of the Web. Also, each search engine has unique ranking algorithms. So when your results are ranked for relevancy, different pages may be at the top of the different lists of results.

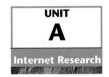

Adding Keywords

The most common mistake people make when searching the Internet is using too few keywords to adequately describe a topic. In fact, most people enter a single keyword when performing a search, which typically returns thousands, if not millions, of search results. Choosing the number of keywords that enable you to locate information quickly and easily is often a trial-and-error process. ▰▰▰▰ You want to locate more specific information on developing solar energy for Portland, so you decide to add some keywords to your search. You also want to find out whether adding keywords really improves your search results, so you decide to start with a basic search term, then add to it.

STEPS

QUICK TIP

Your browser should be open and the Searching the Internet document should be open in your word processor.

1. **Go to the Online Companion at** www.course.com/illustrated/research3, **then click the** MSN Search link **(under "Search engines")**

   The search form for MSN Search opens.

2. **Click in the** Search text box **if necessary, type** solar energy, **then click** Search

   Your screen should look similar to Figure A-9. A count of the total results appears just below the Search text box, and is followed by list of sponsored links and then the first page of results.

3. **In the** Adding Keywords table **in your document, record how many results this search found**

   The number of results is quite large and the page descriptions are not particularly relevant to using solar energy as an alternative power source for a city. You decide to add the keyword "city" to your query.

4. **In the Search text box, click after the keyword** energy, **press** [Spacebar], **type** city, **then click** Search

   Your screen should look similar to Figure A-10.

5. **In the same table in your document, record how many results this search yielded**

   This search returns far fewer results. In addition, the page descriptions indicate that the information is more closely related to solar energy use in a city.

6. **In the Search text box, click after the keyword** city, **press** [Spacebar], **type** develop, **then click** Search

   The number of results is now even smaller and more closely related to how to develop solar energy for a city, so they are the most useful for your purposes.

7. **In the same table in your document, record how many pages this search found, then save your changes to the document**

FIGURE A-9: MSN search for *solar energy*

Your search

Number of results

Your results

Keywords highlighted in results

Help link

Sponsored results

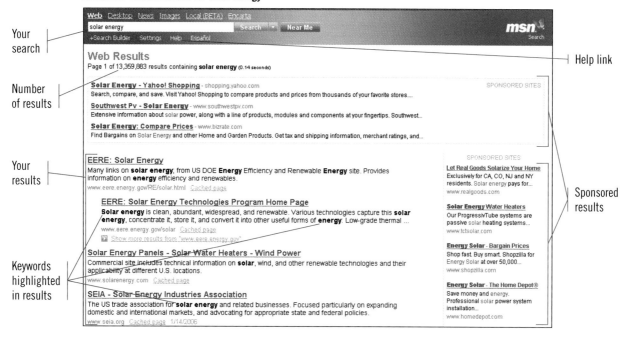

FIGURE A-10: MSN search for *solar energy city*

Your search

Number of results

Your results

Sponsored results

Keywords highlighted in results

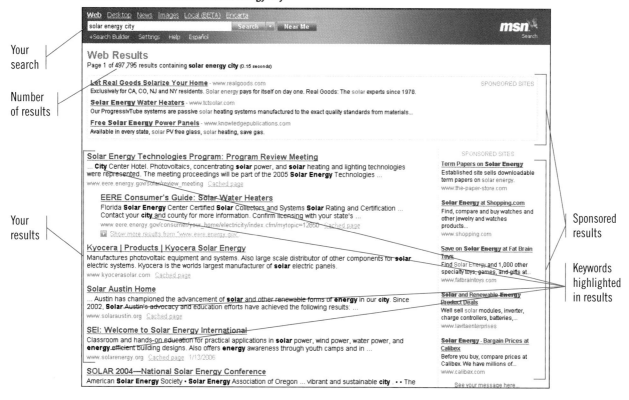

Clues to Use

Arranging keywords

The order in which you place keywords in a search can be very important. Placing your most important keywords at the beginning of your search query causes a search engine to display documents featuring the more important keywords at the top of your search results. For example, the keywords *hybrid electric vehicle* cause a search engine to first look for documents containing the word

"hybrid," then "electric," and, finally, "vehicle." Reversing the order of this search query (that is, *vehicle electric hybrid*) puts less emphasis on the keywords "hybrid" and "electric," hence changing the sequence of your search results. Depending on the search engine's algorithms, it might also change the number of your search results.

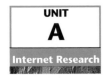

Phrase Searching

When you construct a search with more than one keyword, you often need two or more words to be in a sentence one right after the other. For example, some pages that happen to contain the words "solar" and "energy" aren't actually about "solar energy." To find these words in the correct order, you need to phrase search. In many search engines, **phrase searching** is accomplished by putting quotation marks (" ") around the words you want to appear together in your results. ▰▰▰ Bob suggests that your multi-key-word searches can be refined even more with phrase searching. You want to have the most meaningful results returned, so you decide to try some phrase searches and compare the results.

STEPS

1. **Go to the Online Companion at** www.course.com/illustrated/research3, **then click the** Google link **(under "Search engines")**
   The search form for Google opens.

2. **Click in the** Google Search text box, **type** bioenergy center, **then click** Search

3. **Record the number of results in the** Phrase Searching table **in your document**

> **QUICK TIP**
>
> Be creative and try variations in your searches, especially when using a search engine for the first time. You can discover a great deal about how the search engine functions by experimenting and then recording the number and quality of your results.

4. **Delete the previous query in the Google Search text box, type** center bioenergy, **then click** Search

   You should have approximately the same number of results as in your previous search. If *center bioenergy* and *bioenergy center* find close to the same number of results, you know that you have not limited your search to just the phrase *bioenergy center*. In a tool indexing millions of pages, this test's results can vary by a larger number than when using a tool such as a subject guide, which would be more likely to return identical results.

5. **Use the same table in your document to record the number of results**

   You now use phrase searching to limit your results.

6. **Delete your previous query in the Google Search text box, type** "bioenergy center", **then click** Search

   Be sure to type quotation marks around the words *"bioenergy center"* to tell Google that you mean to search for an exact phrase. You should now have far fewer results than in the first two searches. You have now located only the Web pages that contain the exact phrase *bioenergy center*. Figure A-11 compares both of the two word searches with the phrase search. Figure A-12 illustrates the results for the phrase search.

7. **Use the same table to record your results, then save your document**

FIGURE A-11: Comparing two-word searches with a phrase search

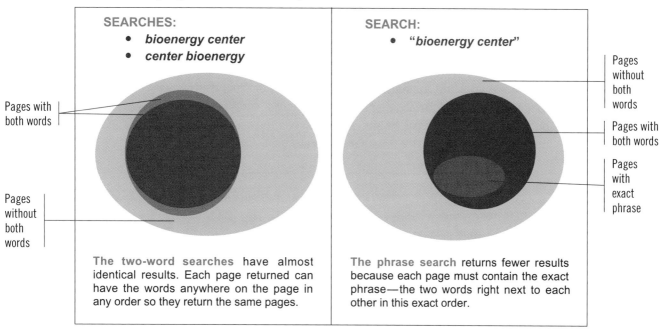

SEARCHES:
- *bioenergy center*
- *center bioenergy*

SEARCH:
- *"bioenergy center"*

Pages with both words

Pages without both words

Pages without both words

Pages with both words

Pages with exact phrase

The two-word searches have almost identical results. Each page returned can have the words anywhere on the page in any order so they return the same pages.

The phrase search returns fewer results because each page must contain the exact phrase—the two words right next to each other in this exact order.

FIGURE A-12: Google phrase search *"bioenergy center"*

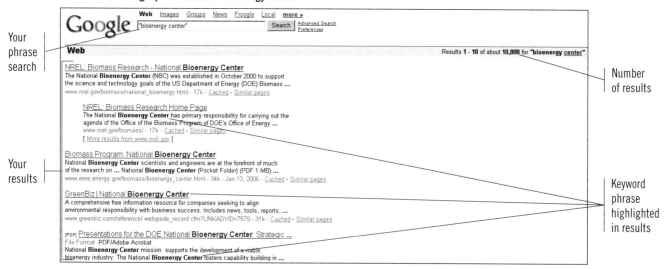

Your phrase search

Your results

Number of results

Keyword phrase highlighted in results

Clues to Use

Other ways to search using phrases

Most search engines allow phrase searching, but not all in the same way. Many use quotation marks around words to indicate a phrase. However, some might automatically assume you are looking for a phrase when you enter two words in the Search text box, in which case quotation marks are redundant, but harmless. Some search engines might provide a drop-down menu or check box with an option for "exact phrase." Others might include an additional Search text box labeled "with this exact phrase." Sometimes the option for a phrase search might appear on an advanced search page. Use the Help or Search Tip pages at each search engine to learn how it uses and interprets phrase searching.

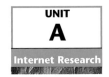

Analyzing Search Results

As you search, you need to scan the results pages to identify Web sites that seem most likely to be useful. Search results pages offer clues that can help you zero in on the best results. Knowing how to navigate and read the results page can save you time as you select from your search results. Figure A-13 points out how to note many of the following examples in your results. ▨▨▨▨ Bob has conducted a search using Google on the keyword *geothermal*. He sits down with you to analyze the search results and uses the following guidelines in determining the quality of the results.

DETAILS

QUICK TIP

As you search, you will become familiar with domain names. For academic information, look for .edu sites. For sites that sell or advocate, look for .com and .org. For professional or association sites, look for .org. For government sites, look for .gov.

- **Locate your search terms within the search result**

  Search engines often display snippets of text from the pages containing your keywords. The number of times your keywords show up in the snippet might indicate the relevance of the Web page to your search. The proximity of the words can also indicate relevance, as would a keyword in the URL. Google displays your search terms in bold for easy scanning.

- **Decipher the URL**

  The name of a URL is often **mnemonic;** that is, it indicates what the Web site is about so that its URL is easier to remember. If the URL contains one of your keywords, it is likely to be mainly about your topic. The end of the domain name (.com, .edu, .jp, .uk, and so on) indicates either a certain type of Web site or its geographic domain. If a URL ends in .gov, it is a page sponsored by a government agency. If a URL ends in .uk, it is from the United Kingdom. Being aware of this as you scan your results can be very helpful. A search for *domain names* or *country domains* results in lists you can check URLs against.

QUICK TIP

If you want to find the one site Google thinks is the "best," click the I'm Feeling Lucky button. This is usually the first non-sponsored result.

- **Note the result's ranking in the list of possible Web pages**

  Search engines use **algorithms**, or mathematical formulas, to rank each Web site according to the terms used in your search query. Every search engine has a slightly different algorithm for figuring out which is the "best" Web site, but all place their best picks at the top of the list. Generally speaking, you shouldn't have to go through more than several pages of search results to find several useful pages. If you do, try refining your search.

- **Determine if the search engine uses directory links**

  More and more search engines are creating directories (or subject guides) of recommended Web sites on many subjects. If a search engine site has included a Web page in its directory, it might indicate relevance. Clicking a directory link sends you directly to that category of Web pages.

- **Determine if the search engine uses cached pages**

  Sometimes links to Web pages break. Search engines might not become aware of the problem until their spiders search that part of the Web again. As a result, sometimes when you click a link you get a computer error message. Google has many hidden, or **cached**, copies of indexed Web pages. If you click the word "Cached," you see the copy of the Web page with your keyword(s) highlighted, as shown in Figure A-14. Cached pages can help you find the newer or renamed or relocated version of the page, or find authors' names or other specific terms. Try a new search query using those terms to look for a new location for this site.

- **Navigate between search results pages**

  Search results are usually displayed about 10 to a page. Some searches return hundreds of pages. At Google you navigate to a different page of results using the links located at the bottom of each results page, as shown in Figure A-15. Google, as well as some other engines, also offers search-refining options at the bottom of the page of results.

FIGURE A-13: Evaluating a search results page

Your search

Highest ranking results have the keyword in the title, the URL, and on the page

Mnemonic URL

Keyword in URL

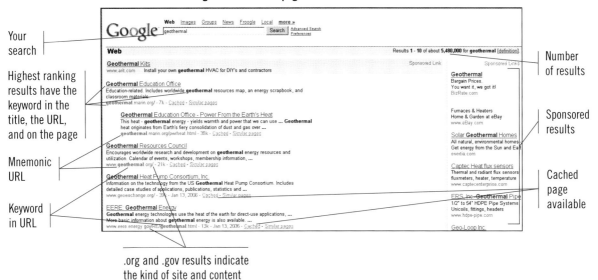

Number of results

Sponsored results

Cached page available

.org and .gov results indicate the kind of site and content

FIGURE A-14: Google's cache of a page from Harvesting Clean Energy

Google's notification that this is a cached page

Your search

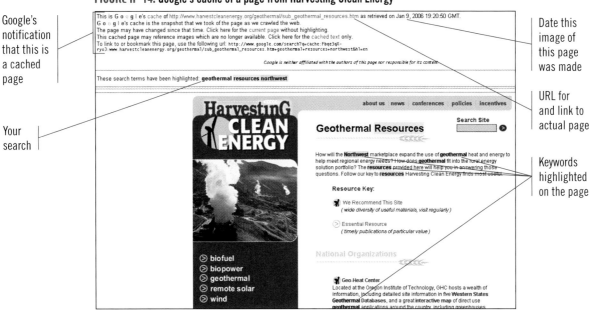

Date this image of this page was made

URL for and link to actual page

Keywords highlighted on the page

FIGURE A-15: Bottom of Google search results page

Search in limited book downloads *(may require registration)*

More pages of search results *(best results should be on the first few pages)*

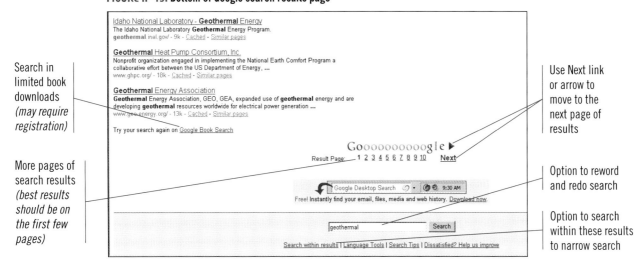

Use Next link or arrow to move to the next page of results

Option to reword and redo search

Option to search within these results to narrow search

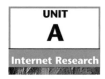

Citing Online Resources

When you use information from Web pages for class work, you need to list them in your works cited. Even if your research is not for school, it is a good idea to gather enough information about each Web page so that you, or someone reading your work, can find it later. To present the relevant data about each site consistently, use a recognized citation format. **Citation formats** are style guides that standardize how citations are written. Two widely accepted citation formats are those of the Modern Language Association (MLA) and the American Psychological Association (APA). These style guides provide formats for all kinds of Internet information. See Table A-3 for citation tips. For school work, always check with your instructor to see which style guide format is preferred. Bob advises you to use the MLA format to record citations for the Web pages you are finding in a way that will make your list consistent and easy for you or your colleagues to find again.

STEPS

> **QUICK TIP**
> To learn more, go to the Online Companion at www.course.com/illustrated/research3 for citation guide links, under "Other Resources."

1. **Review Figure A-16, which shows the elements of an MLA citation**

   Figure A-17 shows an example MLA citation, and Figure A-18 shows the Web site cited in the example.

2. **Locate the author named in Figure A-18, then type the name in the Citing Online Resources table in your document**

   MLA format for author names is surname (last name) first, followed by a comma, then the personal name (first name) followed by a period. Note that many Web pages do not display this information as clearly as the example. You might have to look to find it and it might not be provided at all.

3. **Locate the title of the Web page in Figure A-18 and type it in the same table**

   MLA format requires quotation marks around the title with a period at the end of the title.

4. **Find the title of the Web site and type it in the same table**

   MLA format requires the title be underlined and followed by a period.

5. **Look for the date the Web page was created or the date it was last updated**

   As in Figure A-18, sometimes there is no creation/update date and you must skip this step.

> **QUICK TIP**
> The URL for any Web page is visible in the browser's address bar.

6. **Type http://science.howstuffworks.com/solar-cell.htm in the same table in your document**

   The URL should be enclosed in angle brackets < > and should not be underlined.

7. **Type the date that you are viewing this Web page in the same table**

   MLA format for dates is *DD Month Abbreviation YYYY* followed by a period. For example: 15 Oct. 2006. It is important to record the date you view a Web page because pages are changed frequently.

> **QUICK TIP**
> Be sure to use all of the required punctuation.

8. **Compare your citation to the example in Figure A-17, make corrections as needed, then save, print, and close the document**

Clues to Use

Copyright and plagiarism

With the exception of works in the public domain, everything on the Internet is copyrighted, whether it is a Web page, an image, or an audio file. If you want to profit from someone else's work, you must get permission from the author or creator. Copyright law is very complex, so consult a lawyer who specializes in copyright law. If you want to use part of someone else's work in a school assignment or paper, you generally can do so under the Fair Use exemption to copyright law. "Fair use" allows students and researchers to copy or use parts of other people's work for educational purposes. Always give credit by citing the source of the material you are using. If you don't credit an author or source, you are guilty of plagiarism. For more information, see "Other Resources" in the Online Companion.

FIGURE A-16: MLA citation format for a Web page

Author Last Name, Author First Name.
"Web Page Title."
Web Site Title.
Date site created or revised.
<Full Internet address>
Date you viewed the Web page.

FIGURE A-17: MLA style citation for Web page shown in Figure A-18

Aldous, Scott.
"How Solar Cells Work."
Howstuffworks.
<http://science.howstuffworks.com/solar-cell.htm>
15 Oct. 2006.

FIGURE A-18: Web page cited in Figure A-17

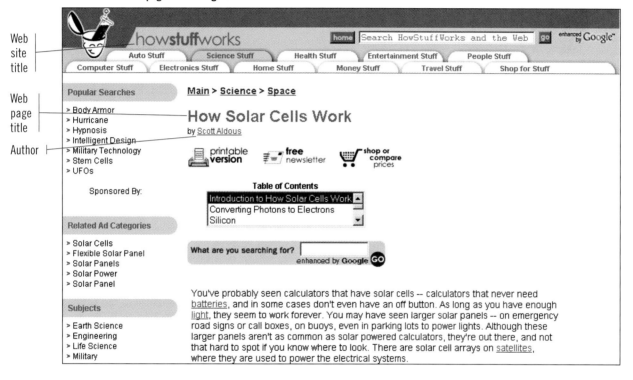

TABLE A-3: Citation tips

citation section	tips
Author	• When authors aren't named, skip this section • If a corporate author is named, such as an association, institution, or government agency, use it in the author section
Page title	• Sometimes the title is not clear; it might be under a banner or logo at the top of the page • If you are citing the whole Web site, you can skip this section, which is for a specific page
URL	• The URL should not be underlined • Some word processors automatically underline URLs, so you might need to remove the underline
Date created/revised	• Sometimes a date can be difficult to find; it might be at the very bottom of the page • When dates aren't provided, skip this section
Date viewed	• If you print the page, the date is at the lower-right corner of your printout • If you are not printing, note the date for your citation

Practice

▼ CONCEPTS REVIEW

Label each element of Figure A-19.

FIGURE A-19

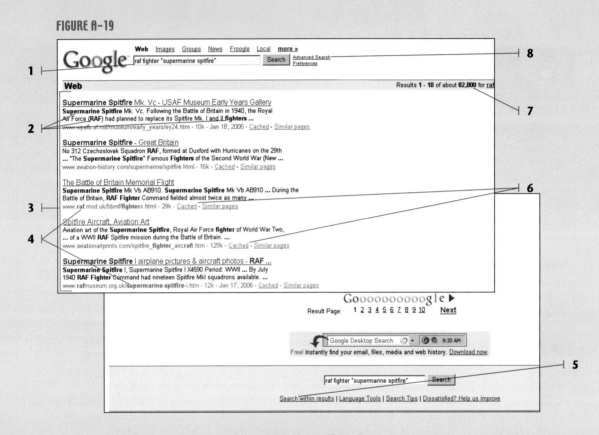

Match each term with the statement that best describes it.

9. **Result's ranking**
10. **Cached page**
11. **Search engine**
12. **Keywords**
13. **Sponsored links**
14. **Search tools**
15. **Synonyms**

a. A Web site that locates information on the Internet by searching Web pages
b. Words that describe your search topic
c. Web pages that have paid for higher placement on search result pages
d. The order in which a search tool returns results, usually based on relevancy
e. A copy of a Web page stored by a search engine
f. Words that have similar meanings
g. A service that helps you find information on the Internet and the Web

Select the best answer from the list of choices.

16. **Which is *not* a step in the recommended Internet research strategy?**
    a. Defining your research topic
    b. Choosing the proper Internet search tool
    c. Entering keywords without preparation
    d. Evaluating your search results

17. **Phrase searching helps you find:**
   a. Words in the order you specify.
   b. Keywords.
   c. Wildcards.
   d. Synonyms.

18. **Which is *not* part of an MLA citation for a generic Web page?**
   a. Author's first name
   b. Web page title
   c. City from which Web page is published
   d. URL

19. **Where is it best to put the most important keyword in your search?**
   a. Anywhere in your search query.
   b. At the beginning of your search query.
   c. At the end of your search query.
   d. The order of the keywords does not make any difference.

▼ SKILLS REVIEW

1. **Understand Internet search tools.**
   a. Open the file IR A-2.doc from the drive and folder where your Data Files are located, save it as Internet Searches in the *YourName* folder where you are saving files for this book, then type your name in the space provided.
   b. In the Skill #1 box in your document, write a paragraph describing the four common Internet search tools.
   c. Save your document.

2. **Create an Internet research strategy.**
   a. In the Skill #2 table in your document, type the seven steps of an effective Internet research strategy in order.
   b. Write a paragraph below the steps explaining the importance of translating your topic into a search query and the value of refining your query to retrieve better results, then save your document.

3. **Identify the right keywords.**
   a. You have defined your search topic as follows: I want to find information about the history of cotton farming.
   b. Type the topic in the Skill #3 table in your document.
   c. Boldface or underline the three keywords in the topic and list them below the topic.
   d. Think of at least three synonyms or related words for the keywords (they might all be for the same keyword).
   e. Type the synonyms and related words next to the appropriate keywords in your document, then save your document.

4. **Perform a basic search.**
   a. You have decided to search for cotton plantations.
   b. Go to the Online Companion at www.course.com/illustrated/research3, then click the Google link.
   c. Perform the search cotton plantations, record the total number of results in the Skill #4 table in your document, then save it.

5. **Add keywords.**
   a. You need information about museums covering cotton plantations and gins.
   b. Go the Online Companion, then click the Google link.
   c. Perform the search cotton plantation and record the number of relevant results that appear on your first page of results in the Skill #5 table in your document.
   d. Add the keyword gin, perform this search, and in the same table record the number of relevant results on your first page of results.
   e. Add the keyword museum, perform this search, in the same table record the number of relevant results on your first page of results, then save your document.

6. **Phrase search.**
   a. Go to the Online Companion, then click the Google link.
   b. Search for the phrase "cotton plantations".
   c. Use the Skill #6 table in your document to record the number of search results, then save your document.

7. **Analyze search results.**

   a. Go to the Online Companion, then click the Google link.

   b. Search for **cotton**, then record the total number of results in the Skill #7 table in your document.

   c. In the same table, record the number of results on the first page of results that contain your keyword.

   d. Record the number of results that have paid to be listed on the first page of results.

   e. Record the number of results on the first page of results that Google has cached.

   f. Record whether Google displays your search term in bold in each result, then save your document.

8. **Cite online resources.**

   a. Select one of the Web pages returned by one of your cotton-related searches.

   b. Print the page you plan to cite.

   c. In the Skill #8 box, create an MLA format citation for the page.

   d. Save, print, and close your document, then exit your word-processing program.

▼ INDEPENDENT CHALLENGE 1

You want to find information on George Harrison's use of the sitar in the song Norwegian Wood. You decide to use phrase searching to narrow your search results.

   a. In your word processor, create a new document, type your name at the top, then save it as **Harrison** in the *YourName* folder where you are saving files for this book.

   b. Go to the Online Companion at www.course.com/illustrated/research3, then click the Google link.

   c. Perform the search **george harrison norwegian wood**, then record the number of results in your document.

   d. Perform the search **"george harrison" norwegian wood**, then record the number of results in your document.

   e. Perform the phrase search **"george harrison" "norwegian wood"**, then record the number of results in your document.

   f. In your document, type a few sentences describing your results and explaining why the phrase search found fewer results.

Advanced Challenge Exercise

- Perform the search **"George Harrison" sitar**, then record the number of results in your document.
- Perform the search **"George Harrison" sitar "World Music"**, then record the number of results in your document.
- Perform the search **"George Harrison" sitar "World Music" audio**, then record the number of results in your document.
- For the search **"George Harrison" sitar "World Music" audio**, record the number of results on the first page of results that contain one of your keywords or keyword phrases in the title.
- For the same search, record the number of results on your first page of results that are from the domain .uk.
- For the same search, if any result on your first page of results mentions an audio clip in its description, note the first part of its URL in your document.

   g. Save your document, print it, close it, then exit your word-processing program.

▼ INDEPENDENT CHALLENGE 2

Your friend is considering a career change and wants you to help with a Web search. The topic statement is: I want to find information about careers in computing in Great Britain.

   a. Start a new document in your word processor, save it as **UK Computing** in the *YourName* folder where you are saving files for this book, then type the topic statement at the top of the page.

   b. Boldface or underline the keywords in the topic.

   c. Copy each keyword onto a separate line.

▼ INDEPENDENT CHALLENGE 2 (CONTINUED)

d. Adjacent to each keyword, type relevant synonyms and related words.

e. From all of your keywords, compose a search and type it on the next line (include one phrase in the search).

f. Go to the Online Companion at www.course.com/illustrated/research3, then click the Yahoo! link.

g. Perform your search, then record the number of search results in your file.

h. Add your name to the document, save it, print it, close it, then exit your word-processing program.

▼ INDEPENDENT CHALLENGE 3

You want to search the Internet for information on a topic of your choosing.

a. Decide on a topic and describe it in a sentence.

b. Decide on the keywords, synonyms, and related terms.

c. Develop a basic search query, choose a search engine, and perform a search.

d. Analyze the search results using the skills you learned in this unit.

e. Print the first page of results and write your name at the top.

f. In your word-processing program, create a new document, save it as **My Topic** in the *YourName* folder where you are saving files for this book. In the document, describe how you analyzed your results.

g. Create an MLA citation for one of your resulting pages, then save your document.

Advanced Challenge Exercise

- Perform the search **wwii**, then record the number of results in your document.
- Perform the search **"wwii"**, then record the number of results in your document.
- Perform the search **"wwii" supermarine spitfire**, then record the number of results in your document.
- Perform the search **"wwii" "supermarine spitfire"**, then record the number of results in your document.
- Perform the search **"wwii" "supermarine spitfire" battle of britain**, then record the number of results in your document.
- Perform the search **"wwii" "supermarine spitfire" "battle of britain" "september 15"**, then record the number of results in your document.

h. Add your name to the document, save, print, and close it, then exit your word-processing program.

▼ INDEPENDENT CHALLENGE 4

You decide to choose a topic and compare search results of the same search using two different search engines.

a. Create a new document in your word-processing program, then save it as **Two Search Engines** in the *YourName* folder where you are saving files for this book.

b. Choose a topic, develop a topic statement, then type the topic statement in your document.

c. Identify the keywords, synonyms, and related terms, then record them in your document.

d. Choose one keyword and search for it using two different search engines of your choice.

e. Record the number of results from each search.

f. Choose a keyword phrase from your previous search results and perform the phrase search in the same two engines.

g. Using the Help pages, read about searching at both engines.

h. In the same document, describe how the search engines and their results pages are different or similar.

i. Add your name to the document, save, print, and close it, then exit your word-processing program.

Internet Research

▼ VISUAL WORKSHOP

A friend gives you a printout of the Web page shown in Figure A-20, but the URL that should be at the bottom of the page is torn off. You decide to find the page from the information on the printout. Using a search engine of your choice, search for the page. Create a new document in your word-processing program, then save it as **Hockey** in the *YourName* folder where you are saving files for this book. Record the citation for this Web page in MLA format. Save, print, and close the document, then exit your word-processing program.

FIGURE A-20

Constructing Complex Searches

OBJECTIVES

Understand Boolean operators
Narrow a search with the AND operator
Expand a search with the OR operator
Restrict a search with the AND NOT operator
Use multiple Boolean operators
Search with filters
Combine Boolean operators and filters
Use metasearch engines

In the previous unit, you learned how to perform a basic search using keywords and phrases. Many search engines also allow complex search queries, which are usually called advanced searches and for which special text boxes are provided. A **complex query** uses special connecting words and symbols called Boolean operators to define the relationships between keywords and phrases. **Boolean operators**, such as AND, OR, and AND NOT, let you expand, narrow, or restrict searches based on Boolean logic. **Boolean logic**, or Boolean algebra, is the field of mathematics that defines how Boolean operators manipulate large sets of data. Because search engines handle large data sets, most support Boolean logic and complex query statements. **Search filters** provide another method to narrow your search by limiting its scope to a specific part of the Web. Combining complex query statements with search filters lets you conduct complex or advanced searches that focus more exactly on your target. You can also use a metasearch engine to search multiple search engines' indexes simultaneously to retrieve broad search results. The city planning team reviews the results from your searches on solar energy as an alternative energy resource. They now want information on area solar energy associations, the use of solar energy by surrounding states, and information on wind energy. To help you design search strategies to meet their requests, Bob provides information on Boolean operators and filters you can use to refine your searches.

Understanding Boolean Operators

The English language has a set of rules, or **syntax**, for combining words to form grammatical sentences. Many search engines rely on a special mathematical syntax, called Boolean logic, for constructing complex queries. In Boolean logic, keywords act like nouns in a sentence. Like nouns, keywords represent subjects. Boolean operators work like conjunctions in a sentence, and define the connections between keywords. Boolean logic is usually illustrated with Venn diagrams. ▰▰▰▰▰ Bob provides the following information on Venn diagrams to help you understand how to use Boolean operators to develop more precise searches. He explains that you'll be better able to create complex searches after you understand how Boolean operators connect keywords.

DETAILS

To review Boolean operators and Venn diagrams:

- ### Venn diagrams

  Venn diagrams are drawings that visually represent searches using Boolean operators. For example, consider the Venn diagrams in Figure B-1. The rectangle represents the World Wide Web. Circles inside the rectangle represent groups of related Web pages, called **sets**. One circle represents a search for pages containing the word *cats*. Another circle represents a search for *dogs*. If the circles overlap, the overlapping area represents pages that are retrieved by both searches. This overlapping area is called the **intersection** of the sets. If you limit your search to pages containing *both* the words, the search results are represented by the intersection of these two circles. If you expand your search to pages containing *either* word, the search results are represented by both full circles. This is called the **union** of the two sets. If you restrict your search to pages containing one word, but *not* the other one, this search is represented by the part of one circle that does *not* overlap the other one. This search excludes one set from the other. Table B-1 shows how the searches illustrated by the Venn diagrams are entered and interpreted.

- ### Common Boolean operators: AND, OR, and AND NOT

  The most common Boolean operators are the words AND, OR, and AND NOT. They act as commands to the search engine by connecting the keywords and phrases it uses to retrieve the results you want. They tell the engine which keywords *must* be on the Web page (AND), which *may or may not* be on the Web page (OR), and which keyword *must not* be on the Web page (AND NOT).

- ### Default Boolean operator

  Search engines insert Boolean operators into multiple word searches whether supplied in the search query or not. The operator that the engine automatically uses is called the **default operator**. Most search engines default to AND. Others default to OR. When you search two or more words, some engines assume you want the words in a phrase and treat the query as if you used quotation marks. Being aware of an engine's default operator is important to create the best search strategy for that engine.

- ### Where to use Boolean operators

  Some search engines allow Boolean searching on the basic search page, but some allow it only on the advanced search page. In the past, almost all search engines recognized all Boolean operators when typed in all capital letters in the Search text box on the basic search page. Now many only recognize them if you use the advanced search page's specialized text boxes. Some do not allow the use of the English words AND or NOT, but do allow the plus sign (+) or minus sign (–) instead.

Clues to Use

Keeping a search diary

Boolean search statements provide a standardized way of noting your searches. It is a good idea to log searches as you perform them, noting the Boolean operators. This helps you remember what searches you have tried and which ones yielded useful results. Your search logs can also be used by others to reproduce your search results.

FIGURE B-1: Venn diagrams illustrating Boolean logic

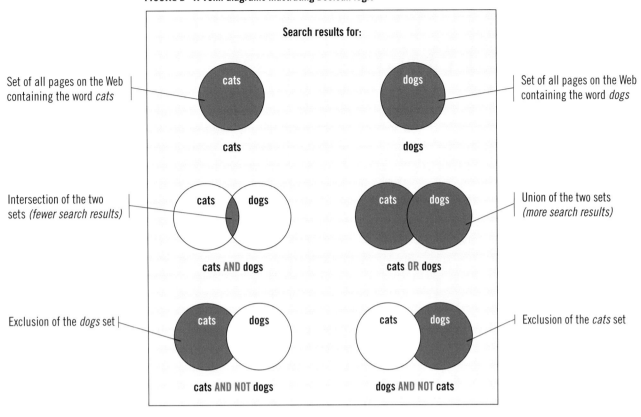

Search results for:

Set of all pages on the Web containing the word *cats* — cats / cats

Set of all pages on the Web containing the word *dogs* — dogs / dogs

Intersection of the two sets *(fewer search results)* — cats AND dogs

Union of the two sets *(more search results)* — cats OR dogs

Exclusion of the *dogs* set — cats AND NOT dogs

Exclusion of the *cats* set — dogs AND NOT cats

TABLE B-1: How the searches represented in Figure B-1 might be entered in and interpreted by a search tool

search	operator	search interpreted as asking for
cats	-	Web pages containing the word *cats*
dogs	-	Web pages containing the word *dogs*
cats dogs	**AND**	Web pages containing both words (AND is the assumed operator in most search tools so you rarely type it)
cats OR dogs	**OR**	Web pages containing either word
cats -dogs	**AND NOT**	Web pages containing the word *cats* but not the word *dogs*
dogs -cats	**AND NOT**	Web pages containing the word *dogs* but not the word *cats*

Clues to Use

Where have you heard this before?

You might remember Boolean logic and Venn diagrams from a math class. George Boole (1815–1864), an Englishman, invented a form of symbolic logic called Boolean algebra, which is used in the fields of mathematics, logic, computer science, and artificial intelligence. John Venn (1843–1923), also an Englishman, used his diagrams to explain visually what Boole had described symbolically—the intersection, union, and exclusion of sets. Little did they know then that they were creating the foundation of the language that Internet search engines use today.

Narrowing a Search with the AND Operator

The Boolean operator AND is a powerful operator that limits your results. Whenever you connect keywords in your search with AND, you are telling the search engine that *both* of the keywords must be on every Web page, not just one or the other. Each AND added to your search query further narrows the search results to fewer pages. However, these pages will be more relevant than those returned by a broader, or less specific, search. A good time to use AND is when your initial keyword or phrase search finds too many irrelevant results. Table B-2 provides more information on the AND operator. ▰▰▰▰ Bob reminds you to be aware that most search engines now use AND as their default operator. This means that actually entering AND between your keywords is unnecessary because the engine assumes you mean to connect keywords with AND unless you tell it otherwise. Bob explains that to search for solar energy associations near Portland, you can use the AND operator to narrow your search, even though you will not literally be typing AND between your keywords.

STEPS

1. **Start your word-processing program, open the file** IR B-1.doc **from the drive and folder where your Data Files are located, save it as** Complex Searches **in the** *YourName* **folder where you are saving files for this book, then type** your name **at the top of the document**
   You can use this document to record your search results.

2. **Start your browser, go to the Online Companion at** www.course.com/illustrated/research3, **then click the** Google link **(under "Search engines")**
   The Google Basic Search page opens.

QUICK TIP
Don't forget the quotation marks, which show that you want your keywords searched as a phrase.

3. **Type** "solar energy association" **in the Google Search text box, then click** Google Search

4. **Use the** Narrowing a Search with the AND Operator table **in your document to record the number of search results**
   Noting the number of results illustrates how Boolean operators can broaden or narrow a search.

QUICK TIP
You do not have to capitalize proper names in search text boxes.

5. **Delete the first search in the Google Search text box, type** portland **in the Google Search text box, then click** Search

6. **Record the number of search results in the same table in your document**
   To find the pages that contain *both* the name *Portland* and the phrase *"solar energy association"* you would have to read as many Web pages as these two resulting sets combined. But you realize you can create a search strategy using a Boolean operator to identify these pages for you.

QUICK TIP
If you were to add a third keyword with the AND operator, you would get *fewer* results because AND narrows your search. So, fewer results are returned for: "solar energy association" AND Portland AND "passive solar."

7. **Delete the search in the Google Search text box, type** "solar energy association" portland, **then click** Search
   This search, using the assumed AND operator, narrows your results to *solar energy association* pages that also contain *Portland*. Figure B-2 is a diagram of this search. Figure B-3 illustrates the search results. This search is meant to make you aware of how using the Boolean operator AND affects your results. Most search engines use AND as the default operator now, so you rarely need to enter it. Instead, you just enter your keywords and the ANDs are assumed.

8. **Record the number of search results in your document, then save the document**

FIGURE B-2: Venn diagram illustrating results for the search "solar energy association" AND Portland

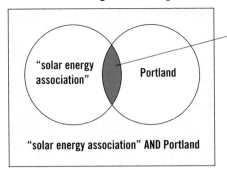

Web pages containing both "solar energy association" AND Portland (the intersection of the two sets)

"solar energy association" AND Portland

FIGURE B-3: Google search: "solar energy association" AND Portland

Your search

Number of results

How your search was interpreted and searched by Google

TABLE B-2: The Boolean operator AND

why/when to use	• When finding too many irrelevant results • To narrow, limit, or focus a search • To force the search of a stop word
variations	• Usually unnecessary because most search engines assume AND • AND • + (the plus sign)
searches	• Most basic searches allow either + or AND, but its use is not required • Most advanced searches provide a specialized text box (or check box or list box) often labeled "with all of the words" or "must include"
sample uses /results	• **use:** *solar panels*; **result:** assumed AND between keywords narrows search and returns fewer results • **use:** *+the hypercar*; **result:** forces inclusion of the stop word "the"

Clues to Use

Using the plus sign: +

The plus sign is usually not required to represent the Boolean operator AND. When you enter more than one keyword, AND is assumed by most search engines. However, you still might encounter some search tools in which you have to use + or AND. You will know by checking the tool's Help page.

The plus sign is very useful to prevent a search engine from ignoring a stop word. For example, *Henry +I* produces the same results as *"Henry I."* The plus sign functions like quotation marks around a phrase. Whether using quotes or +, you are forcing the search engine to look for a word it would normally ignore.

When you use the plus sign, you must leave a space in front of it, but no space between it and the keyword it is connecting to the first keyword. Examples: *+the goal orr* (used to force inclusion of a stop word); *music +blues +memphis* (used as the Boolean AND).

Expanding a Search with the OR Operator

As you have seen, the AND Boolean operator *narrows* your search. Conversely, the Boolean operator OR *expands* your results. When you connect keywords in your search with OR, you are telling the search engine to list every Web page that contains any of the keywords. In other words, every page returned must have at least one of the keywords on it but it doesn't need to have more than one. Each OR added to your search expands the search to include more Web pages. A good time to use OR is when your initial search finds too few results. Refer to the synonyms or related words you identified when developing your search strategy and connect one or more to your search with OR. Table B-3 provides more information about the OR operator. ▰▰ Your city planning team requested that you find information on wind energy. Checking your list of synonyms and related words, you decide to perform a complex search using OR to connect the keyword phrases "wind energy" and "wind turbines."

STEPS

TROUBLE

If your browser is not at Google, go to the Online Companion at www.course.com/ illustrated/research3, then click the Google link.

1. **At the Google site, type** "wind turbines" **in the Google Search text box, then click** Search
   Before performing your Boolean OR search, you want to search the keywords alone to compare results.

2. **Use the** Expanding a Search with the OR Operator table **in your document to record the number of search results**

3. **Delete your previous query in the Google Search text box, type** "wind energy", **then click** Search

4. **Use the same table in your document to record the number of search results**
   Now you want to compare these results to a search connecting the two search phrases with the OR operator.

QUICK TIP

If you were to add a third keyword with the OR operator, you would get more results, because OR broadens your search. So, more results are returned for: "wind energy" OR "wind turbines" OR "wind mills."

5. **Delete your previous query in the Google Search text box, type** "wind energy" OR "wind turbines", **then click** Search
   Figure B-4 illustrates your search results with a Venn diagram. This search combines the results of both of your previous searches. Figure B-5 shows Google's search results page. Numbers of results change all the time, so don't expect yours to match the figure. You might reasonably expect the number of results to be significantly higher than it is, because the OR expands the search. It is somewhat lower than expected because some Web pages contain both phrases and the results page eliminates many duplicates. This search is meant to make you aware of how using the Boolean operator OR affects your results.

6. **Record the number of search results in your document, then save your document**

FIGURE B-4: Venn diagram illustrating results for the search "wind turbines" OR "wind energy"

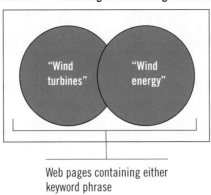

Web pages containing either
keyword phrase

FIGURE B-5: Google search: "wind energy" OR "wind turbines"

Your
Search

Keyword
phrases
highlighted
in your
results

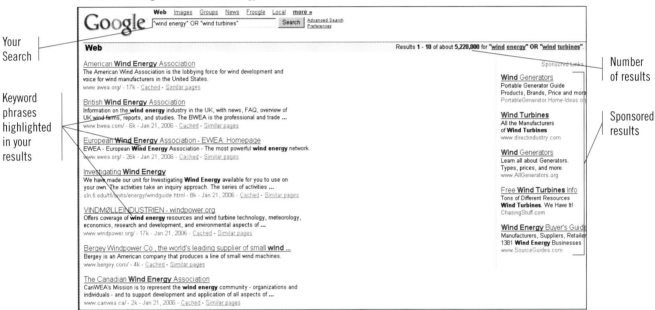

Number
of results

Sponsored
results

TABLE B-3: The Boolean operator OR

why/when to use	• When finding too few results • To broaden a search • To combine synonyms or related terms
searches	• Most basic searches allow OR • Most advanced searches provide a specialized text box (or check box or list box) labeled "with any of the words" or "with at least one of the words"
sample uses/ results	• **use:** *oregon* OR *northwest*; **result:** broadens search and returns more results • **use:** *renewable* OR *sustainable* OR *alternative*; **result:** combines related words and requires that only one be on any one page

Restricting a Search with the AND NOT Operator

The Boolean operator AND NOT excludes the keyword or phrase that follows it. Therefore, AND NOT narrows or limits your search. When you add AND NOT and an additional keyword to a search strategy, fewer results are returned. Use the AND NOT operator if your initial search returns too many irrelevant results. When you scan the first couple of results pages and see numerous irrelevant pages returned, try to locate any words or phrases that your desired search results should *not* contain. This is a good time to identify a category of results you do *not* want to retrieve and add it to your search with AND NOT. Table B-4 provides more information about using AND NOT. 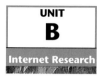 You have been reviewing your search results for solar energy associations in Portland. You notice they include Web pages about two cities—Portland, Oregon, and Portland, Maine. You are only interested in associations in Portland, Oregon. You show your problem to Bob, who explains the easiest way to deal with this might be to search with the phrase "Portland Oregon." However, he suggests, to practice with the Boolean AND NOT logic, that you conduct another search using the AND NOT operator to eliminate pages referring to Portland, Maine. This way you will not only eliminate pages mentioning Maine, but will also have returned to you pages that contain Portland that might not contain Oregon. Before trying AND NOT, you decide to search without it to compare results.

STEPS

1. **At the Google site, clear the** Google Search text box **if necessary, type** "solar energy association" Portland, **then click** Search

   Again, the results include Web pages about both cities—Portland, Oregon, and Portland, Maine.

2. **Use the** Restricting a Search with the AND NOT Operator table **in your document to record the number of search results**

   Now you want to use AND NOT to exclude Web pages about Portland, Maine. In Google, you must use the minus sign (–) for the Boolean operator AND NOT.

3. **Click immediately after the word** Portland **in the Google Search text box, press** [Spacebar], **type** Oregon -Maine, **then click** Search

   Be sure to not leave a space between the minus sign and the word *Maine*. When using the minus sign (–), there must always be a space in front of it and no space between it and the next keyword. Figure B-6 shows a Venn diagram of your search. Your results should look similar to Figure B-7.

4. **Use the same table to record the number of search results, then save your document**

> **QUICK TIP**
> If you were to add a third keyword with the AND NOT operator, you would get fewer results because AND NOT narrows your search. So, fewer results are returned for: "solar energy association" AND NOT Maine AND NOT Oregon.

Clues to Use

More on the AND NOT operator

You might encounter the AND NOT Boolean operator referred to as AND NOT, ANDNOT, NOT, and most often as the minus sign (-). However it is written, the Boolean logic is the same—it excludes the following word or phrase from the search results. When you use the minus sign (-), include a space before it but do not leave a space between it and the word it is connecting to in the search query. So, a search for *cats* AND NOT *dogs* retrieves the same results as the search *cats -dogs*. A search tool's Help pages should provide information about how it understands Boolean operators.

FIGURE B-6: Venn diagram illustrating results for the search "solar energy association" AND Portland AND NOT Maine

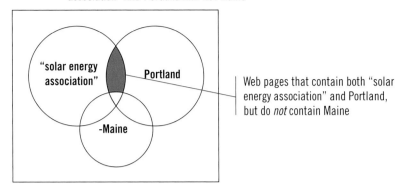

Web pages that contain both "solar energy association" and Portland, but do *not* contain Maine

FIGURE B-7: Google search "solar energy association" AND Portland AND NOT Maine

Your search

How your search was interpreted and searched

TABLE B-4: The Boolean operator **AND NOT**

why/when to use	• To focus or narrow or limit a search • To exclude a keyword • When finding too many irrelevant results
variations	• Hyphen or minus sign (-) is the most commonly used • You might also encounter AND NOT, ANDNOT, or NOT
searches	• Most basic searches allow the minus sign (-) • Most advanced searches provide a specialized text box (or a check box or list box), labeled "must not include" or "without the words"
sample use/result	• **use:** *"alternative energy" -geothermal*; **result:** excludes the word geothermal and returns fewer results

Using Multiple Boolean Operators

Combining Boolean operators in your search strategy provides even more focused results. You can use operators in any logical combination. When searching with more than one set of keywords, use parentheses to tell the search tool which words belong together. When using more than one operator, use parentheses to force the order in which the search is performed. Unless the query instructs search tools to do otherwise, the query is read and the operators are performed from left to right. When you use parentheses, you instruct the search tool to perform the part of the search inside the parentheses first. This is called **forcing the order of operation**. Using parentheses has a significant impact on search results. Figure B-8 illustrates results in which the search tool read the query and performed the search from left to right, producing irrelevant results. Figure B-9 illustrates results in which the order of operation was forced, producing relevant results.  In your last team meeting, you agreed to find information on solar energy resources from the surrounding region, not just in Portland, Oregon. Bob suggests you combine Boolean operators in a complex search. First, you want to search two sets of keywords separately so you can compare results.

STEPS

1. **At the Google site, clear the** Google Search text box **if necessary, type** "Washington state" OR "British Columbia" OR "Pacific Northwest", **then click** Search

   You learned on previous searches that if you just enter *Washington* your results contain many pages referring to Washington, D.C., so you included the word *state*. Your results appear.

2. **Use the** Using Multiple Boolean Operators table **in your document to record the number of search results**

3. **Delete your previous query in the Google Search text box, type** "solar energy", **click** Search, **then use the same table in your document to record the number of search results**

   Now you need to combine and limit these results to Web pages about solar energy that also refer to the Northwest, but do not refer to Oregon. You use parentheses to tell Google which sets of words belong together.

4. **Click in the** Google Search text box, **edit your search to read** "solar energy" ("Washington state" OR "British Columbia" OR "Pacific Northwest") -Oregon, **then click** Search

   Remember that you must use the minus sign (–) for Google to understand you mean AND NOT. Figure B-10 illustrates your results in a Venn diagram.

5. **Use the same table in your document to record the number of search results, then save your document**

Clues to Use

Using multiple Boolean operators in basic and advanced search forms

Most search tools contain advanced search pages, which can be convenient for putting together complex searches. If you ever find yourself unsure about what to do when using these pages, return to these basic tools: identifying keywords and related words, sketching Venn diagrams to recall how the Boolean operators work, and writing down your search strategy using the Boolean operators AND, OR, and AND NOT. Just as understanding the mathematical functions that are being performed by the calculator that you use for convenience helps you successfully exploit your calculator, understanding Boolean logic helps you create successful online search strategies when you use the convenience of advanced search pages. However, the more complicated your complex searches become, the more likely you will need to go back to the basic search page where you have more control over your search statement.

FIGURE B-8: Venn diagram illustrating the search: constitution American OR "United States"

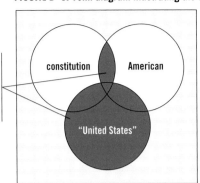

Order of operation *was not* forced with parentheses, so the search engine read the operators from left to right, resulting in Web pages containing constitution and American and then OR "United States"

FIGURE B-9: Venn diagram illustrating the search: constitution (American OR "United States")

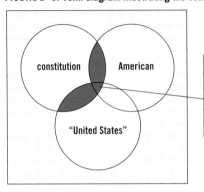

Order of operation *was* forced with parentheses, so the part of the search inside the parentheses was read first, resulting in Web pages containing constitution and then either American or "United States"

FIGURE B-10: Venn diagram illustrating the search: "solar energy" ("Washington state" OR "British Columbia" OR "Pacific Northwest") -Oregon

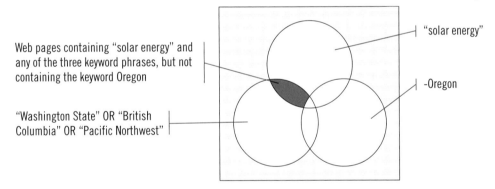

Web pages containing "solar energy" and any of the three keyword phrases, but not containing the keyword Oregon

"Washington State" OR "British Columbia" OR "Pacific Northwest"

"solar energy"

-Oregon

Clues to Use

Planning a complex search

You can combine Boolean operators to develop a complex search strategy. For example: If you want to use Google to search alternative energy in British Columbia or Alberta, Canada, but do *not* want pages on geothermal energy, here are sample steps to develop an effective strategy:

1. Identify the first concept. Use keywords, synonyms, and related words. Connect them with OR and surround them with parentheses.

   (British Columbia OR BC OR Alberta)

2. Identify the second concept. Use keywords/synonyms/related words, and connect them with OR and surround them with parentheses.

   (Canada OR Canadian)

3. Identify the third concept. Quotation marks identify this as a phrase.

   "alternative energy"

4. Identify the fourth concept. You want this word excluded from your results, so you use the Boolean operator AND NOT. Google uses the minus sign (–) as AND NOT.

   –geothermal

5. Connect all of your concepts into one search statement.
   (British Columbia OR BC OR Alberta) AND (Canada OR Canadian) AND "alternative energy" -geothermal

Searching with Filters

Another way to refine a search is to use filters. **Filters** are programs that tell search tools to screen out specified types of Web pages or files. They are usually located on advanced search pages. As you develop your search strategy, use filters to search only a specified area of the Web or to exclude specified areas of the Web. For example, you use language filters to search only for pages in English, or date filters to search only for pages updated in the last year, or for certain file types such as images, audio, or video. Table B-5 lists examples of filter options available on Google's Advanced Search page. One of your team members read that Denmark is a leader in wind power. You want to see some Danish sites, but because you don't read Danish, you need to find pages that are in English. Bob suggests you use filters on an advanced search page to focus the search. He tells you that the domain for Denmark is .dk.

STEPS

QUICK TIP

For more complex Boolean searches, it is usually more efficient to use the Basic Search page. This reduces the chances of inadvertent logic errors.

1. **At the Google site, click** Advanced Search, **then click your browser's** Refresh button **to clear the text boxes if necessary**

   The Google Advanced Search page includes a number of convenient options to simplify constructing Boolean searches involving only a few keywords or phrases.

2. **Click the** Language list box, **then click** English

   See Figure B-11. With this filter, your search results will only include Web pages written in English. Now you want to restrict your search to the domain exclusive to Denmark.

QUICK TIP

The Domains filter lets you choose between "Only return results from the site or domain" or "Don't return results from the site or domain." In this search, you want it to read Only.

3. **Type** .dk **in the Domain text box**

   See Figure B-11. With this filter, your search results will only include Web pages from Denmark.

4. **Type** wind power **in the with the exact phrase text box, then click** Search

   Quotation marks are not needed to indicate a phrase search. This specialized text box interprets any words typed here as a phrase, so quotation marks are assumed. Figure B-12 illustrates the results in a Venn diagram. The Web pages returned contain the phrase *wind power*, are in English, and are from Denmark's domain.

5. **Use the** Searching with Filters table **in your document to record the number of search results, then save your document**

   Note that Google has translated your search as *"wind power" site:.dk*. Quotation marks show how Google interpreted the words you typed into the "with the exact phrase" box. The *site:.dk* is how Google translated your domain filter selection. Just below the tabs you see that Google searched only pages in English. Google reiterates your query as Searched *English* pages for *"wind power" site:.dk*. Check this information to determine if the filters worked the way you expected when you developed the search strategy.

TABLE B-5: Commonly used filters on Google's Advanced Search page

Language	Limits search to pages written in the language you choose (English, French, Japanese, etc.)
File Format	Limits search to pages in the format you choose (.pdf, .xls, .doc, etc.)
Date	Limits search to pages updated within a specified time period (3, 6, or 12 months)
Occurrences	Limits search to pages containing your keywords in the location you choose (URL, title, links, etc.)
Domain	Limits search to include pages only with a specified domain or to exclude pages with a specified domain
SafeSearch	Limits search by filtering to exclude potentially offensive pages (can be hit and miss)

FIGURE B-11: Boolean logic and filters on Google's Advanced Search page

Phrase search for "wind power"

Language filter with English selected

Domain filter with .dk entered

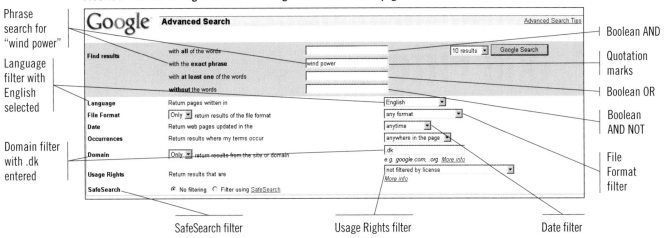

Boolean AND

Quotation marks

Boolean OR

Boolean AND NOT

File Format filter

SafeSearch filter

Usage Rights filter

Date filter

FIGURE B-12: Venn diagram for: "wind power" domain:.dk language: English

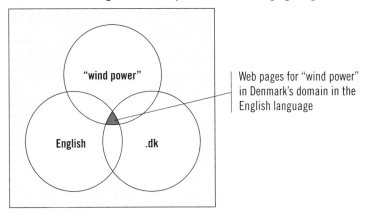

Web pages for "wind power" in Denmark's domain in the English language

Clues to Use

Filtering domains in the URL

Filters search only for letters or words that appear in certain parts of a URL. The final two or three letters in the URL indicate domains. Web sites in the United States have URLs that end in three letters that represent the type of organization hosting the Web site. For example: university sites end in .edu; government sites end in .gov; commercial sites end in .com; and nonprofits end in .org. Others include: .biz, .pro, .info, .net, .us, .coop, .museum, and .name. Web sites located in other countries use two-letter country codes: Canada's domain is .ca; the United Kingdom's domain is .uk; Japan's domain is .jp. Any of these two- or three-letter codes can limit search results when using a domain filter. For a full listing of the two-letter country codes, go to www.iana.org/cctld/cctld-whois.htm. You can find other sites with this information by searching for *countries* AND *domains*.

Combining Boolean Operators and Filters

Most search tools provide advanced search pages that make entering complex searches easier. These pages allow you to combine Boolean operators and filters to create complex, very specific searches that return relevant results. See Table B-6 for an example of planning a complex search strategy. ▨▨ As discussed with your city planning team, you want to identify some Canadian pages on alternative energies. You don't need pages on geothermal energy and, because they will be easy to print and share, you want pages that are in a PDF format. You are not sure how to formulate such a specific query, so you ask Bob for advice. He guides you in developing a strategy utilizing both Boolean operators and filters.

STEPS

1. **At the Google site, click** Advanced Search, **click in the** with all of the words text box, **then type** university energy

   As you saw in the last lesson, Google provides special text boxes for Boolean searching and mostly list boxes for searching with filters. This text box represents the AND Boolean operator.

2. **Click in the** with at least one of the words text box, **then type** alternative sustainable renewable

   This text box represents the OR Boolean operator. You do not need to type the OR.

3. **Click in the** without the words text box, **then type** geothermal

   This text box represents the AND NOT Boolean operator. You do not need to type the AND NOT.

4. **Click the** Language list arrow, **then click** English

   This list box filters for Web pages written only in the language you choose.

5. **Click the** first File Format list arrow, **click** Only, **click the** second File format list arrow, **then click** Adobe Acrobat PDF (.pdf)

   This filters for Web pages that are only in the file format you choose.

6. **Click the** Domain filter list box, **click** Only, **then type** .ca in the Domain text box

   This filters for Web pages that are only located in the domain you choose; .ca is the domain for Canada.

7. **Compare your settings to those shown in Figure B-13, then click** Search

   Your results should appear similar to Figure B-14. Notice that near the top of the page Google restates your search. A quick check of this information verifies the Boolean text boxes and the filters worked as you expected.

8. **Use the** Combining Boolean Operators and Filters table **in your document to record the number of search results, then save your document**

> **QUICK TIP**
>
> Even with a fast Internet connection, you might notice that a complex search using several different operators and filters sometimes takes longer to return results.

Clues to Use

Using the search text boxes on an advanced search page

When using advanced search text boxes, you do not actually type the Boolean operators. When using these specialized text boxes, the search engine understands the operator you want to use so you can enter multiple words without the operators. However, if you need to enter a phrase in the OR box, you need to include quotation marks around the phrase and type a plus sign (+) in front of the words inside the quotation marks. The first word in each phrase does not require the plus sign, but you might want to make a practice of using it in front of any word in a phrase to help you remember a plus sign is needed on every word after the first word. For example, to search for *solar panels* OR *wind turbines* on Google's Advanced Search form, enter: "+solar +panels" "+wind +turbines" in the OR box. This ensures your search is interpreted as two phrases rather than four words. This is an example of why, when your complex searches get more complicated, it is often preferable to go back to the basic search form.

FIGURE B-13: Google Advanced Search page using Boolean logic and filters

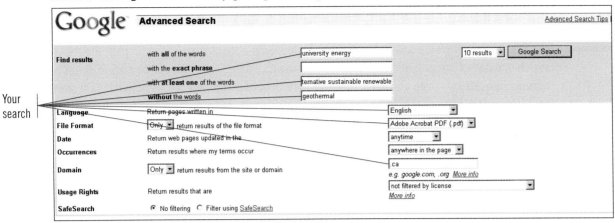

FIGURE B-14: Filters and operators advanced search results

TABLE B-6: Planning a complex search using both Boolean operators and filters

You want to identify some Canadian domain pages, in PDF format, on alternative energies other than geothermal. To use Google for this search, here are the steps to develop your strategy combining Boolean operators and filters:

1. Identify the first concept. Connect keywords with OR and surround them with parentheses.	(alternative OR renewable OR sustainable)
2. Identify the second concept. Use keywords/synonyms/related words, and connect them with OR and surround them with parentheses.	(energy OR energies)
3. Identify the third concept.	-geothermal
4. Use filters as needed.	Language: English Domain: .ca File Format: .pdf

One way to record your search strategy:

      (alternative OR renewable OR sustainable) (energy OR energies) –geothermal site:.ca filetype:.pdf lang:.eng

Using Metasearch Engines

Until now, each of your searches has used a single search engine. Even with complex searching, you only search one part of the Web at a time with a single search engine. If a single search engine doesn't deliver the number or quality of results you need, or if you want to quickly compare results from different search engines to decide which to use for a particular search, you might want to try a metasearch engine. **Metasearch engines** do not search the Web itself; rather they search search engines' indexes. By searching more than one search engine's index simultaneously, metasearch engines often access more of the Web in a single search. However, metasearch engines often do not search the best search engines, because of the fees such search engines charge. Also, search engines that are busy with too many other searches at the exact moment you conduct your search are sometimes skipped, so results can be inconsistent. ▓▓▓▓ While searching for information on alternative energy resources, you have become intrigued with geothermal energy. Bob suggests a simple search on this topic using a metasearch engine.

STEPS

1. **Go to the Online Companion at www.course.com/illustrated/research3, then click the Ixquick link (under "Metasearch engines")**
   The Ixquick Search page opens, as shown in Figure B-15.

> **QUICK TIP**
> The metasearch engine's results are broad, but often not as deep as a single search engine's. A metasearch engine is a good place to start when you want to check the first few results from several search engines.

2. **Click in the Search text box, type "geothermal energy", then click Search**
   Your search is now simultaneously sent to multiple search engines. Ixquick, along with IncyWincy, is one of only a few "smart" metasearch engines, which translate search commands, like quotation marks, into queries that other search engines understand. If you cannot tell whether the metasearch engine you are using does this, stick with very simple searches.

3. **Scroll through the results, noting the features of Ixquick's results: the ranking stars, the Highlighted Results, and the list of search engines after each result showing which engines returned each result**
   Figure B-16 illustrates the Ixquick search results. Ranking stars are used to rank the results by relevance. The Highlighted Result link takes you to a copy of the Web page that highlights your keywords for easy scanning. Ixquick also shows how each engine ranked pages and which results are sponsored.

> **QUICK TIP**
> The Highlight option provides a copy of the Web page that Ixquick has at its site. It is not the original. This copy can be useful if the original site is temporarily down.

4. **Scroll down, if necessary, then click the word Highlight**
   This copy of the Web page highlights the keywords from your search query. This feature can help you quickly determine how useful the Web page might be and if you want to go to the page itself.

5. **Record the number of matching results in the Using Metasearch Engines table in your document; save, print, and close the document; then exit your word-processing program**

Clues to Use

Maximizing metasearching

To effectively use a metasearch engine, always read its Help pages. Help should let you know how "smart" the engine is in translating specific search commands into queries that other search engines understand. With this information, you know if you need to use quotation marks to indicate a phrase. If you're not sure how smart the metasearch engine is, use simple searches consisting of only a few keywords. Also, because the search engines used by a metasearch engine change regularly, note which engines are being used when you perform your search and which are returning the most useful results. Which search engines' indexes a metasearch engine searches can change often. You can usually find where one is currently searching by checking its Help pages or advanced search pages.

FIGURE B-15: Ixquick metasearch search form

Other search options

Advanced search link

Your search

FIGURE B-16: Ixquick metasearch results

Your search

Suggestions for other searches

Search results

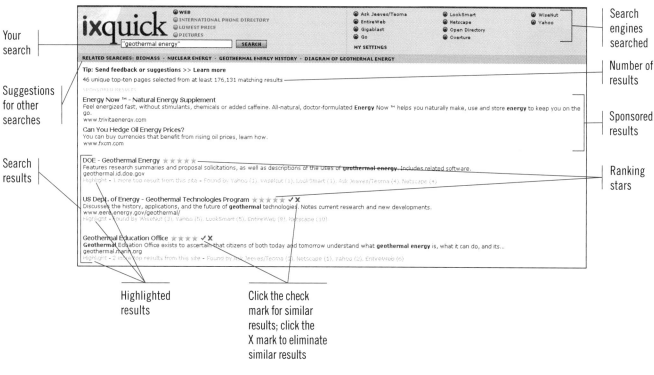

Search engines searched

Number of results

Sponsored results

Ranking stars

Highlighted results

Click the check mark for similar results; click the X mark to eliminate similar results

Practice

▼ CONCEPTS REVIEW

Each of the following Venn diagrams represents searches. The dark color represents the search results. Write out the search for each diagram.

FIGURE B-17

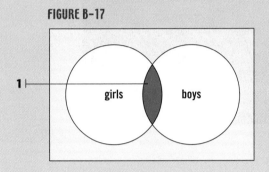

1

FIGURE B-18

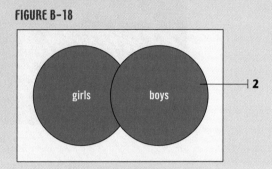

2

FIGURE B-19

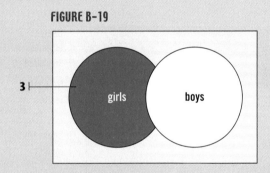

3

FIGURE B-20

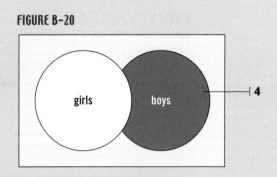

4

Match each term with the statement that best describes it.

5. **Boolean operators**
6. **Venn diagrams**
7. **AND operator**
8. **OR operator**
9. **AND NOT operator**
10. **Metasearch engines**
11. **Parentheses**
12. **Filters**
13. **Algorithm**

a. A way to visualize how Boolean operators work

b. Is used to connect synonyms

c. A mathematical formula used by search engines to rank search results

d. Aids to screen out unwanted Web pages

e. Force the order of operation in a Boolean search

f. Is used to exclude words from a search query

g. One way to narrow a search

h. Indicate how keywords are to relate to each other in a search query

i. A search engine that searches multiple search engines rather than the Web itself

Select the best answer from the list of choices.

14. The place where two search result sets overlap is called the _____ of the two sets.
    a. Union
    b. Combination
    c. Intersection
    d. Margin

15. Each Boolean operator AND that links another keyword to your search finds:
    a. More Web pages.
    b. Exactly the same number of Web pages.
    c. Fewer Web pages.
    d. None of the above.

16. Equivalent wording for the Boolean OR in an advanced search list box might be:
    a. Either of the words.
    b. All of the words.
    c. None of the words.
    d. Must not contain.

17. Which is *not* a standard variation of the Boolean operator AND NOT?
    a. NOT
    b. The hyphen or minus sign (–)
    c. NOT MORE
    d. ANDNOT

18. Which is *not* a potential downside to using metasearch engines?
    a. Instability
    b. Secrecy
    c. Inconsistency
    d. Usually limited to simple searches

19. If the order of operation in a complex Boolean search is not forced, the search tool:
    a. Reads the query from left to right.
    b. Inserts the parentheses for you.
    c. Returns no search results.
    d. Automatically applies filters to your search.

20. A search tool that doesn't recognize Boolean operators as English words in its basic search:
    a. Cannot be used to search with Boolean logic.
    b. Probably allows Boolean searching from text boxes or list boxes in its advanced search pages.
    c. Sometimes allows the Boolean AND and AND NOT if you use the plus sign (+) and the minus sign (–) instead of words.
    d. b and c

21. The part of a URL that can contain a two-letter country code is the:
    a. File.
    b. File extension.
    c. Domain.
    d. Page.

22. Which is *not* true of all metasearch engines?

   a. The search engines searched can change frequently.

   b. They are a good place to start when you want to see the top results from several engines.

   c. They interpret your search the way every other search engine can understand it.

   d. They might skip searching an engine they normally search if that engine is busy at that moment.

23. Using parentheses in a complex search tells the search engine that:

   a. The part of the search inside the parentheses should be performed first.

   b. The words inside the parentheses should be treated as a subset in the search.

   c. The words inside the parentheses should be excluded from the search.

   d. a and b

▼ SKILLS REVIEW

1. Understand Boolean operators.

   a. Start your word-processing program, open the file **IR B-2.doc** from the drive and folder where your Data Files are located, save it as **Boolean Searches** to the *YourName* folder where you are saving files for this book, then add your name at the top of the page.

   b. Use the Skill #1 table in the document to describe the effects on search results of using each of the Boolean operators: AND, OR, and AND NOT.

2. Narrow a search with the AND operator.

   a. Start your browser, go to the Online Companion at www.course.com/illustrated/research3, then click the Google link.

   b. Perform an initial search on **Mars**.

   c. Use the Skill #2 table in your document to record the number of search results.

   d. Return to the Search page, then edit your search by adding **water**.

   e. Use the same table in your document to record the number of search results.

   f. Edit your AND search again by adding **robots**.

   g. Use the same table in your document to record the number of search results, then save your document.

3. Expand a search with the OR operator.

   a. Go to the Online Companion, then click the Google link.

   b. Perform an initial search on **Mars**.

   c. Use the Skill #3 table in your document to record the number of search results.

   d. Return to the Search page, then edit your search by adding **OR water**.

   e. Use the Skill #3 table in your document to record the number of search results.

   f. Edit your search again by adding **OR robots**.

   g. Use the Skill #3 table in your document to record the number of search results, then save your document.

4. Restrict a search with the AND NOT operator.

   a. Go to the Online Companion, then click the Google link.

   b. Perform an initial search on **Mars**.

   c. Use the Skill #4 table in your document to record the number of search results.

   d. Return to the Search page, then edit your search by adding **-water**.

   e. Use the same table in your document to record the number of search results.

   f. Edit your AND NOT search again by adding **-robots**.

   g. Use the same table in your document to record the number of search results, then save your document.

5. Use multiple Boolean operators.

a. Go to the Online Companion, then click the Google link.

b. Perform an initial search on **Mars robots**.

c. Use the Skill #5 table in your document to record the number of search results.

d. Return to the Search page, then edit your search by adding **(Europe OR Canada)** to the initial search criteria.

e. Use the same table in your document to record the number of search results, then save your document.

6. Search with filters.

a. Go to the Online Companion, click the Google link, then click Advanced Search.

b. Perform an initial search on **Mars**.

c. Filter the results for English.

d. Use the Skill #6 table in your document to record the number of search results.

e. Return to the Search page, filter the search for Web pages updated in the past year, filter the domain for Germany (.de), then perform the search.

f. Use the same table in your document to record the number of search results, then save your document.

7. Combine Boolean operators and filters.

a. Go to the Online Companion, click the Google link, then perform the search.

b. In the AND search text box, type **Mars**.

c. In the OR search text box, type **water geology**.

d. Click the Language list arrow, select English, then perform the search.

e. Use the Skill #7 table in your document to record the number of search results.

f. On the Advanced Search page, click the second File Format list arrow, click Microsoft PowerPoint, then perform the search again. (*Note:* The first File Format list arrow should read "Only.")

g. Use the same table in your document to record the number of search results, then save your document.

8. Use metasearch engines.

a. Go to the Online Companion, click the Ixquick link, then, if it is not already selected, click the Web option button.

b. Perform an initial search on **Mars NASA**.

c. Use the Skill #8 table in your document to record the total number of matching results.

d. Use the same table in your document to record the number of results on the first page of results that are marked for relevancy with three or more stars.

e. Go back to Ixquick's basic search page, click Power Search, then perform the search: **Mars NASA (geology OR water)**.

f. Use the same table in your document to record the total number of matching results.

g. Use the same table to record the number of results on the first page of results that are marked for relevancy with three or more stars.

h. Save your document, print it, close it, then exit your word-processing program.

▼ INDEPENDENT CHALLENGE 1

You want to find Web sites in Russia (domain .ru) about the Hermitage Museum. You don't read Russian so you want the Web pages to be in English.

    a. Use the Online Companion (www.course.com/illustrated/research3) to go to the Google site, then open the Google Advanced Search page.

    b. Set the appropriate filters, then perform your search.

    c. Print out the first page of search results.

    d. Add your name to the top of the printout.

▼ INDEPENDENT CHALLENGE 2

You want to explain to a friend how Boolean operators work. You decide to draw a series of three Venn diagrams to illustrate what happens when using AND, OR, and AND NOT.

    a. Draw a Venn diagram illustrating how the AND operator works and label it "The AND operator."

    b. Draw a Venn diagram illustrating how the OR operator works and label it "The OR operator."

    c. Draw a Venn diagram illustrating how the AND NOT operator works and label it "The AND NOT operator."

    d. Add your name to the top of the page(s).

▼ INDEPENDENT CHALLENGE 3

Your history teacher told you that there is a connection between the Library of Congress and Thomas Jefferson. You decide to search the Internet to learn more about this connection.

    a. Use the Online Companion (www.course.com/illustrated/research3) to go to the AllTheWeb search engine.

    b. Click in the Search text box, then type in two appropriate search phrases using quotation marks.

    c. Scroll through the first page of results and look for a URL with the clickable phrase **more hits from** beside it.

    d. Click this phrase by the link that you decide to check for your information.

    e. Print out the first page of results, then add your name to the top of the page. (*Hint*: If AllTheWeb is not displaying this feature when you do your search, print out the first page of results from your original search.)

Advanced Challenge Exercise

You are curious about the highest-ranked results other search engines might return on your search for Thomas Jefferson and the Library of Congress. Use a metasearch engine that translates your search to other search engines.

    ■ Use the Online Companion to go to Ixquick. Click in the Search text box, enter your search phrases, then perform the search.

    ■ Print the first page of results, then add your name at the top.

    ■ To learn more about how to search on Ixquick, click the link to the Help pages. (*Hint*: Because search engines redesign their pages frequently, you might have to look around the page for this link; if you don't see a Help link, look for an About link or another likely name.)

    ■ Start your word processor, create a new document, save it as **Library of Congress** to the *YourName* folder where you are saving files for this book, then briefly describe two tips you learned from Ixquick's Help pages.

    ■ Add your name to the top of your document, save it, print it, and attach it to your printout of the results page.

▼ INDEPENDENT CHALLENGE 4

You and some friends want to go on an ecologically friendly vacation—or an ecotour. You are interested in all North American destinations, but need the information to be in English.

a. Write your name at the top of a piece of paper, write out the topic and potential keywords, then circle the keywords and keyword phrases.

b. Write out your search strategy to make it easy to enter your query after you get online.
Hint: You should use the Language filter and the search statement should look similar to this:
keyword +("*keyword* +*keyword*" OR *keyword* OR *keyword* OR "*keyword* +*keyword*")

c. Use the Online Companion (www.course.com/illustrated/research3) to go to Google's Advanced Search and perform the search.

d. Print out a copy of the first page of your search results, then write your name at the top of the page.

e. Attach the printout to the paper on which you wrote your topic and keywords.

Advanced Challenge Exercise

While looking over the results for an ecotour in North America, you become fascinated with the idea of an ecotourism trip in either Alaska or Canada, focusing on grizzly bears or polar bears. You decide to restrict your search to find only relevant sites in English.

- Go to Google's Basic Search page, enter your search query, then print the search page showing the query in the search text box.
- Perform the search, then print the first page of results. Add your name at the top of both printouts.
- Return to Google's Advanced Search page, delete your previous search, and enter your new search.
- Print the Advanced Search page showing your search, then perform the search and print the first page of results. Add your name at the top of the printouts.
- On a blank piece of paper, write a sentence or two about which search form, the basic or the advanced, you felt was easier to use for your search and why.
- On the same page, write a sentence comparing the results of both searches.
- Write your name at the top of this page and attach it to your printouts.

▼ VISUAL WORKSHOP

The Web page shown in Figure B-21 is the result of an effective search strategy. By completing the following steps, re-create a search that can find this page.

a. Look at the Web page and choose keywords that you might use to find this page. Write them down on a piece of paper.

b. On the same page, construct a search query that you think can find this Web page.

c. Go to a search engine and perform your search. If you make adjustments in your search as you go, note them on your paper.

d. After you find this Web page, print a copy and attach it to the paper on which you have written your query. (*Note*: If this page no longer exists on the Web, find one containing a quotation on a similar topic.)

e. Add your name at the top of the printout.

FIGURE B-21

Browsing Subject Guides

OBJECTIVES

Understand subject guides
Browse a subject guide
Search a subject guide
Navigate a subject guide
Tap trailblazer pages
Use a specialized search engine
Understand evaluative criteria
Evaluate a Web page

You have seen how a search of the Web can yield thousands, or even millions, of pages. Using Boolean operators in a planned search strategy to limit results can still leave you with more results than you can reasonably review. However, subject guides can help focus your search and are especially helpful when your knowledge of a topic is too limited for you to feel comfortable judging Web sites as you begin searching. A **subject guide** groups information by topic. These topics, typically arranged alphabetically and hierarchically, allow you to acquaint yourself with the breadth and/or depth of a subject. Many subject guides also allow keyword searching. Although subject guides are typically compiled by experts, rather than by software programs such as search engine spiders, you still need to know how to evaluate the sites gathered from a subject guide. 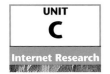 The Portland City Planning team is overwhelmed with the number of Web sites you have found providing information on alternative energy sources. Now they want you to locate very specific information from reliable and credible sources. They particularly want you to focus on renewable energy, geothermal energy, and wind energy. Bob suggests you use subject guides for this phase of the research process.

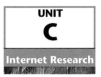

Understanding Subject Guides

Subject guides emphasize quality over quantity. Unlike search engines, subject guides are usually hand compiled and maintained by experts, offering users greater selectivity and quality of information, but less coverage than search engines. These experts often annotate the links to resources with useful information. Carefully designed selection criteria are used to select resources to include in subject guides, which are also known as **subject directories**, **Internet directories**, or **subject trees**. Subject guides organize the sites they index into hierarchical topics that you click your way through, to find relevant links. Links are arranged by subject, like books in a library, for easy access. Subject guides' content varies from general links to mostly commercial to mostly reference or academic links. Table C-1 provides more information about selected subject guides. You want to become more efficient at searching the Web for information on alternative energy. You decide to follow Bob's suggestion to learn more about subject guides.

DETAILS

Some notable characteristics of subject guides are as follows:

- **Organization**

  Subject guides organize links to Web sites into topical hierarchies. A **hierarchy** is a ranked order. The ranked order typically goes from more general to more specific. For example, the general topics (in **bold**) in the Librarians' Internet Index (LII) subject guide, shown in Figure C-1, are followed by related, more specific topics. Clicking a topic, such as "Science," links to a list of subtopics. Subtopics link to increasingly more detailed topics. You navigate or browse a subject guide primarily by "**drilling down**," or clicking through topics and subtopics arranged hierarchically, in increasingly specific subject headings.

QUICK TIP

Differences between subject guides and search engines are disappearing as better guides provide search engines and better engines provide subject categories. Nevertheless, most guides' engines still search only their hand-selected indexes, and most engines' subject categories are still compiled electronically from all sites crawled by their spiders.

- **Selectivity and small size**

  Subject guides are selective. In better subject guides, qualified people rather than computer programs decide which Web pages are worthy of inclusion. Subject guides can provide links to useful sites that search engine spiders are unable to access. They often include **trailblazer pages** or Web pages with links to other sites covering all aspects of a topic. Subject experts also include sites that might cover one or two very detailed subtopics. This kind of selectivity ensures that returned Web pages are some of the best on the subject. Because of this selectivity, subject guides are relatively small, which can be an advantage, saving you the time and trouble of sifting through thousands of search engine results.

- **Access methods**

  In addition to hierarchical lists of topics, better subject guides provide search forms with which you can use keywords to search their indexes. A local search engine allows you to search the titles and the annotations of indexed Web pages. A subject guide might also provide lists of topics arranged in various ways, including alphabetically, geographically, chronologically, or by the Dewey Decimal subject classification system.

QUICK TIP

These annotations are great time-savers, as they provide expert previews of sites for you.

- **Annotations**

  Annotations are summaries or reviews of the contents of a Web page, written by the subject guide contributors, usually experts in the field, such as professionals or academics, or experts in information and the Web, such as librarians. Annotations of Web pages provided by subject guides make subject guides the tools of choice for many researchers.

- **Results**

  Typical subject guide results include the number of results, annotations, and other subject terms under which sites are indexed. The latter can be especially useful when you are just learning about your topic and how it relates to other subjects. Figure C-2 shows a search results display on Librarians' Internet Index (LII).

FIGURE C-1: Librarians' Internet Index (LII) home page

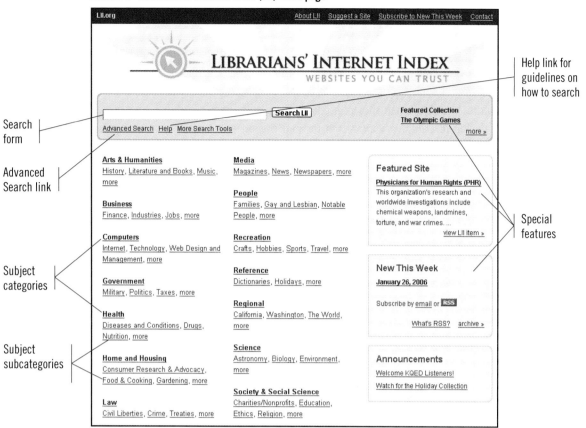

Help link for guidelines on how to search

Search form

Advanced Search link

Subject categories

Subject subcategories

Special features

FIGURE C-2: LII search result

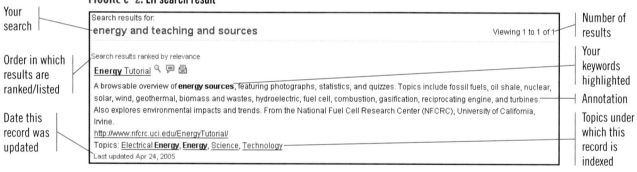

Your search

Order in which results are ranked/listed

Date this record was updated

Number of results

Your keywords highlighted

Annotation

Topics under which this record is indexed

TABLE C-1: Sampling of subject guides (see Online Companion at www.course.com/illustrated/research3)

subject guides	type/pages indexed	features
About.com	General/ some academic/ 1 million +	Very broad, uneven quality, ads
BUBL LINK 5:15	Academic/scholarly/11,000+	Searchable, Dewey #s, UK slant
EERE (Energy Efficiency and Renewable Energy)	Government energy specific/600+ sites/ 120,000 documents	Searchable and drill-down browsing
INFOMINE	Academic/scholarly/distributed/115,000+	Searchable, librarians, high quality
Librarians' Internet Index	General/reference/12,000+	Searchable, librarians, high quality
ipl (Internet Public Library)	General/reference/40,000	Very broad, Univ. of MI, librarians
LookSmart	Commercial/2.5 million	Searchable, mostly .com's
Open Directory	General/3 million	Most search engines use, uneven
Scout Archives	Academic/reference/17,000	Searchable, high quality
WWW Virtual Library	Academic/general/distributed/	Oldest on Web, volunteer indexers

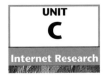

Browsing a Subject Guide

Browsing is the easiest and most effective way to find information in a subject guide. The creators of subject guides review Web sites and organize links to them by topic. By clicking your way through the hierarchy of topics, from the most general to the most specific, you see which sites were deemed best by the guide's contributors. In a distributed subject guide, clicking categories can direct your browser to other sites. You decide to continue your search for information about alternative energy by browsing a few subject guides. Bob highly recommends the Librarians' Internet Index, so you begin there.

STEPS

1. **Start your word-processing program, open the file** IR C-1.doc **from the drive and folder where your Data Files are located, then save it as** Subject Guides **in the** YourName **folder where you are saving files for this book**

> **QUICK TIP**
>
> Topics lead to subtopics.

2. **Go to the Online Companion at** www.course.com/illustrated/research3, **then click the** Librarians' Internet Index (LII) link **(under "Subject guides")**
   Notice there is a search form as well as broad subject categories you can click through to find more specific categories. You decide that your topic, "*alternative energy*," might be under the general heading "Science."

> **QUICK TIP**
>
> A subject guide's list of topics offers numerous choices. If the path you drill down doesn't work, navigate back and try another path.

3. **Click the** Science link
   The resulting page offers numerous science related subcategories, so you need to make a choice.

4. **Click the** Environment link, **then click the** Energy link
   Now you see several more specific categories that should be useful.

5. **Click the** Renewable Energy link, **choose a Web site that looks interesting, then record its title in the** Browsing a Subject Guide table **in your document**
   Figure C-3 shows sites indexed with the phrase "*renewable energy*." This page is the equivalent of a search engine's results page. Notice the results highlight this phrase. You decide to explore another subject guide.

> **QUICK TIP**
>
> If you had entered "*renewable energy*" in the home page search form, this would have been your results page. If you are unsure of keywords, a subject guide helps you identify effective keywords.

6. **Go to the Online Companion, then click the** Open Directory link **(under "Subject guides")**

7. **Click the** Science link, **click the** Technology link, **click the** Energy link, **click the** Renewable link, **click the** Wind link, **then click the** Windmills link
   You have drilled down through over 100,000 results for Science to less than a dozen for Windmills, going from the more general to the more specific. Your end results page should look similar to Figure C-4.

8. **Choose a title that looks interesting, record it in the same table, then save your document**

FIGURE C-3: LII's drill-down results *renewable energy*

Advanced Search link

Drill-down path

Order in which results are listed/ranked

Your results

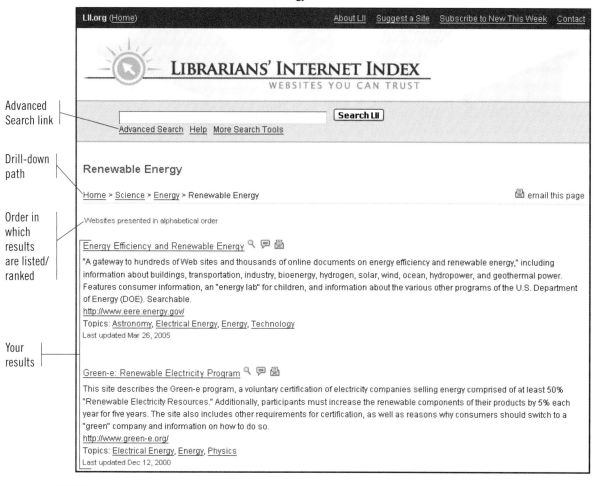

FIGURE C-4: Open Directory's drill-down results *windmills*

Search form

Drill-down path

Related topics

Your results

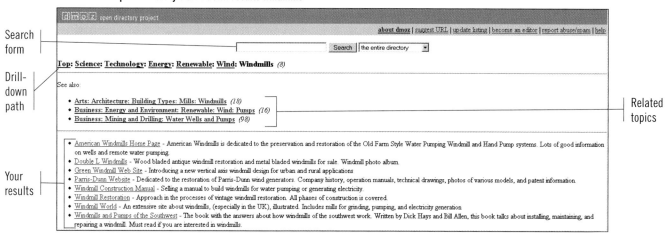

Clues to Use

Distributed subject guides

WWW Virtual Library and the Open Directory Project are examples of distributed subject guides. **Distributed subject guides** are created by a variety of contributors working somewhat independently. Each group or person is usually responsible for a subtopic of a main topic. These guides are said to be "distributed" because rather than being on a subject guide's computer, the Web pages for different parts of the guide are stored on different computers, distributed around the country or around the world. Because distributed subject guides have many contributors working independently, each with varying levels of expertise and resources, distributed subject guides tend to have an uneven quality and a lack of standardization. However, this potential downside is balanced by the fact that these different parts of the guide's index are often maintained by subject experts with a high level of awareness of what is available on the Web in their field.

Searching a Subject Guide

Each subject guide has a unique way of organizing information. As you saw in the preceding lesson, "Energy" might appear under "Science" at one guide and under "Technology" at another. Some subject guides also offer their own local search engine to provide a more direct approach to finding information. Like a regular search engine, a subject guide's local search engine searches its own indexes to return results. The difference is, unlike a Web search engine whose spiders constantly crawl the Web adding the full text of pages to its indexes, a subject guide's index contains only the annotations, keywords, and subject headings assigned to the selected Web pages by the guide's contributors and editors, who are often experts in the field they are indexing. ██████ You want to find more Web sites on geothermal energy, so you decide to try the search engines in the Librarians' Internet Index and Open Directory.

STEPS

1. **Go to the Online Companion at www.course.com/illustrated/research3, click the Librarians' Internet Index (LII) (under "Subject guides"), type geothermal in the Search text box, then click Search**

   Notice that your keywords are highlighted and clickable related subject categories are listed. You decide to try an advanced search.

QUICK TIP

Remember that Web sites redesign their pages frequently. If you don't see an element mentioned in the steps, look around the page for a similarly labeled element.

2. **Click the Advanced Search link (under the Search text box), type geothermal energy northwest in the With all words (And) text box, then click Search**

   Your results should look similar to Figure C-5. They include graphical links for more information on the result, for leaving a comment on the result for the indexers, and for e-mailing the result as well as text links to related subject areas.

3. **Select a site that interests you, then record its title in the Searching a Subject Guide table in your document**

4. **Go to the Online Companion, click the Open Directory (ODP) link (under "Subject guides"), type geothermal energy in the Search text box, then click Search**

   Now you want to try an advanced search.

QUICK TIP

Not all subject guides' advanced searches are as clear as LII's; if it is not clear how a site's advanced search works, it's a good idea to check the Help pages to understand how your search will be interpreted.

5. **Scroll to the bottom of your page if necessary, click the Advanced Search link, type geothermal energy northwest in the Search text box, then click Advanced Search**

   Your results should look similar to Figure C-6. Notice that you are offered the option of repeating your search in numerous other search tools.

6. **Select a site that interests you, record its title in the same table in your document, then save your document**

FIGURE C-5: LII's Advanced Search results *geothermal energy northwest*

Your search

Order in which results are listed

Your results

Click for more information on this record

Click to comment on or e-mail this record

Topics under which this site is indexed by LII.org

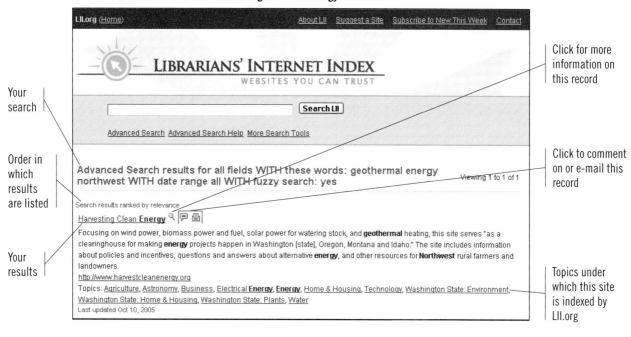

FIGURE C-6: Open Directory's Advanced Search results *geothermal energy northwest*

Your results

Your search

How your search was interpreted

Options to repeat your search in other tools

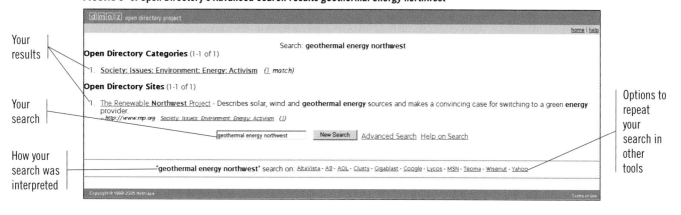

Navigating a Subject Guide

Subject guides might provide hierarchical lists of topics, local search engines, geographical lists, alphabetical lists, or other ways to access the pages in their database. BUBL LINK / 5:15 (BUBL—pronounced *bubble*) also indexes by the Dewey Decimal system, the same numeric subject classification system used in many libraries. ▆▆▆▆ Bob mentions this interesting feature in BUBL and you decide to try it.

STEPS

QUICK TIP

Look at BUBL's URL and note the domain. The .uk domain indicates this site is from the United Kingdom. BUBL has an interesting name; for more information on its meaning, click the About link on the home page.

1. **Go to the Online Companion at** www.course.com/illustrated/research3, **then click the BUBL LINK / 5:15 link (under "Subject guides")**

   The BUBL home page opens, as shown in Figure C-7. You can navigate this subject guide in several ways, including clicking links to Subject Menus, A-Z, Dewey, Countries, Types, and by clicking the broad subject headings. You decide to explore a few of these options.

2. **Click the Subject Menus link at the top of the page, look over the list of subjects, then click the Energy link**

   The alphabetical list of topics under Subject Menus is a way to start clicking through subjects from a more comprehensive list than the broad headings on the home page. The subtopics under "Energy" include their corresponding Dewey Decimal numbers. You decide to click a Dewey number.

QUICK TIP

You can use the descriptions at BUBL to help you determine the authority of a site. If you want further information about an author, search on his or her name.

3. **Click the 333.79 Renewable energy link**

   In its list of sites indexed under 333.79, BUBL provides useful information, including site authors. Now you decide to try the alphabetical index.

4. **On the A-Z links at the top of the page, click the R link, then click the renewable energy link**

   Your results should look similar to Figure C-8. BUBL displays the results two ways: On the left side for easy previewing, BUBL lists the titles, as links, of the Web pages indexed under the term "Renewable energy." To the right, BUBL lists the titles, as well as their annotations and other information, such as their corresponding Dewey numbers. Now you want to try searching by Dewey number.

5. **Near the top of the page, click the Home link**

QUICK TIP

Using BUBL also provides you with an idea how books on your topic might be cataloged in your library.

6. **Click the 300 Social sciences link, on the next page click the 330 Economics link, then click the 333 Environment and economics of land and energy link**

   This page should look familiar. You reached the same page in Step 2 when you navigated the guide using the Subject menus.

7. **Click the 333.79 Renewable energy link, choose one site, record its title in the Navigating a Subject Guide table in your document, then save your document**

   This page should also look familiar. This is the same list you found in Step 3; you just reached it through a different route.

FIGURE C-7: BUBL home page

Search
form

Topics (in
Dewey
Decimal
order)

Subtopics

Ways to
navigate
BUBL

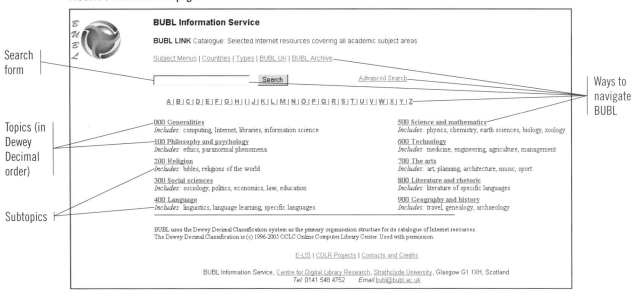

FIGURE C-8: BUBL results *renewable energy*

Your
search

Your
results

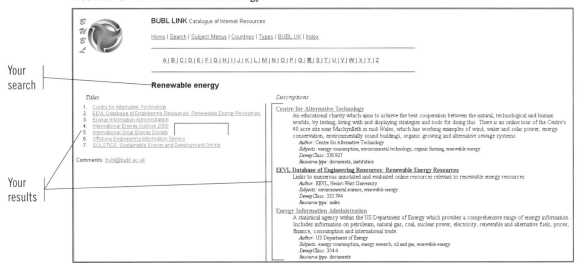

Tapping Trailblazer Pages

The best **trailblazer pages** are Web pages created by scholars, experts, and organizations who seek to organize and provide links to better Web sites in their fields. They are an excellent source of reliable Web resources. These pages can be narrow or broad in scope, but all attempt to provide thorough coverage of their subjects. A good trailblazer page not only provides links to useful sites, but it also provides a logical, well-organized way of navigating them. Organizational features can include a local search engine, user-friendly navigation throughout the site, and a **site map** (an index to the pages on the site). To maximize use of trailblazer pages, you want to familiarize yourself with them. You decide to explore a site Bob recommended—the U.S. Department of Energy's Energy Efficiency and Renewable Energy (EERE) site.

STEPS

TROUBLE
Many Web sites change appearance often. Usually the information remains the same; however, you might need to locate and click slightly different links to find it.

1. **Go to the Online Companion at** www.course.com/illustrated/research3, **then click the EERE link (under "Subject guides")**
   The EERE site opens, as shown in Figure C-9. This site links to over 600 other sites and contains over 120,000 documents at the EERE site itself. Look around the home page, then look for a link that reads "Site Map."

2. **Click the** Site Map link, **then explore this page**
   A site map provides links to access all parts of the site.

3. **Click the** Alphabetical Listing of Sites link
   An alphabetized list of the sites linked from the EERE site opens. Looking at the sites to which a trailblazer page links often provides a clue as to its quality; some pages might be created by devoted fans, hobbyists, or amateurs, and not provide as broad a range of links as one created by a scholar or librarian.

4. **Look over the range of links, then click the** Home link **near the top of the page**
   Now you want to see how the subtopics are organized.

5. **Click the** Biomass link **under Renewable Energy**
   Your screen should look similar to Figure C-10.

6. **In the Search text box, type** "portland oregon", **then click** Search
   Your results, similar to Figure C-11, seem to indicate that EERE is a gold mine of Web resources for your project.

QUICK TIP
Whenever you find a great site, such as EERE, that you know you will want to reference again, save it as a Microsoft Internet Explorer Favorite or a Netscape Bookmark.

7. **Choose one site from your results, record its title in the** Tapping Trailblazer Pages table **in your document, then save your document**

FIGURE C-9: EERE's home page

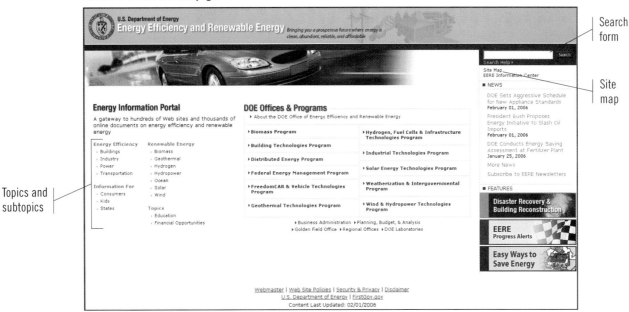

Search form

Site map

Topics and subtopics

FIGURE C-10: EERE's Biomass Topics page

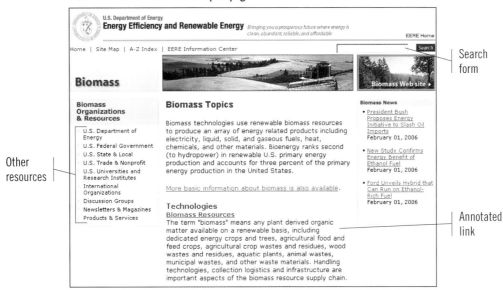

Search form

Other resources

Annotated link

FIGURE C-11: EERE's results *"Portland Oregon"*

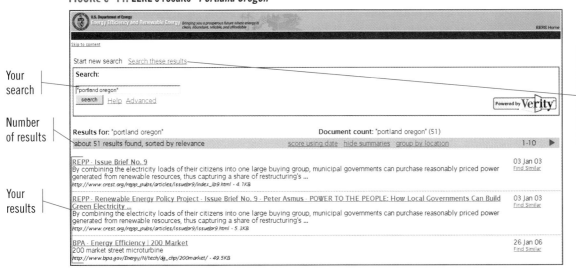

Option to search within current results to narrow results

Your search

Number of results

Your results

Using a Specialized Search Engine

Search engines often find too many results and subject guides might provide fewer than you need. Specialized search engines can combine the best features of both. **Specialized search engines** act similarly to regular Web search engines, except, like some subject guides, they limit the Web pages they search by subject. Specialized search engines are available for a wide variety of topics, including law, medicine, computers, and energy. ▰▰▰ Bob mentions that the specialized search engine, Source for Renewable Energy, is a good place to locate alternative energy resources on the Web. You decide to use it to see if you can find out who sells wind energy equipment in Portland.

STEPS

1. **Go to the Online Companion at www.course.com/illustrated/research3, then click The Source for Renewable Energy link (under "Specialized search engines")**
   The Source for Renewable Energy's home page opens, as shown in Figure C-12. As in other subject guides, there are multiple ways to search, but you want to explore the specialized search engine.

2. **Click the Search the Business Guide link to open the site's specialized search engine**

> **QUICK TIP**
> Remember that you don't need to capitalize proper nouns/names for search tools.

3. **In the Search text box, type "wind energy" "portland oregon", then click Search**
   Make sure to type the two keyword phrases in two separate sets of quotation marks. This guarantees that the search engine interprets your search correctly. Your results page should look familiar—Google provides the search technology for this site. Figure C-13 shows the search results page.

4. **Scroll through the results, noting that each link's URL begins with "energy.sourceguides.com;" click a link that looks interesting; notice the products or services offered and contact information; then record the name in the Using a Specialized Search Engine table in your document**
   The fact that each link's URL begins with the same domain indicates that you only searched this specialized site, not the Web. Now you decide to try accessing this information another way.

5. **Click the Source guides icon at the top of the results page to open the home page**

6. **Click the geographic location link, click the Renewable Energy Businesses in the United States icon, click the Renewable Energy Businesses in the United States by State link, click the Renewable Energy Businesses in Oregon link, click the by Product Type icon, then click the Wind Energy Businesses in Oregon link**
   This is the drill-down method of searching a subject guide. Look at the path you used under the Source Guides icon at the top of the page. Figure C-14 illustrates your results page.

> **TROUBLE**
> If no result has a site, record the name of one of your results.

7. **Look over the results, choose a business that has its own Web page, record the URL in the same table, then save your document**

Clues to Use

How do you find a specialized search engine?
Ask a librarian or instructor if they can recommend a specialized search engine for your research topic. They might also be able to help you identify trailblazer pages, which are good sources of important Web sites in subject areas, such as the ones listed in the Online Companion under the heading "Specialized search engines." Sometimes you will find a link to a specialized search engine in a good trailblazer page or a subject guide.

FIGURE C-12: The Source for Renewable Energy home page

Information about what this subject guide contains

Ways to search

Click to open the specialized search engine

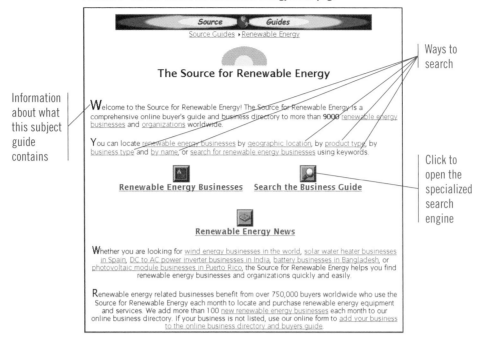

FIGURE C-13: The Source for Renewable Energy search results *"wind energy" "Portland Oregon"*

Your search

Your results

Sponsored results

How your search was interpreted

Number of results

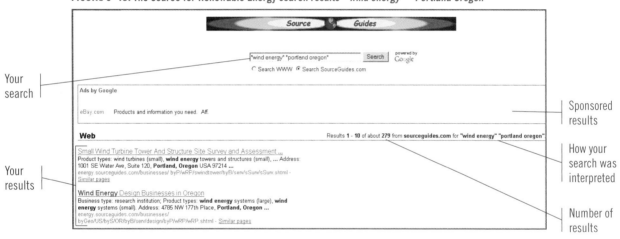

FIGURE C-14: The Source for Renewable Energy drill-down results

Drill-down path

Your search

Sponsored results

Your results

Source guides icon

Related results

Related sponsored results

Sponsored results

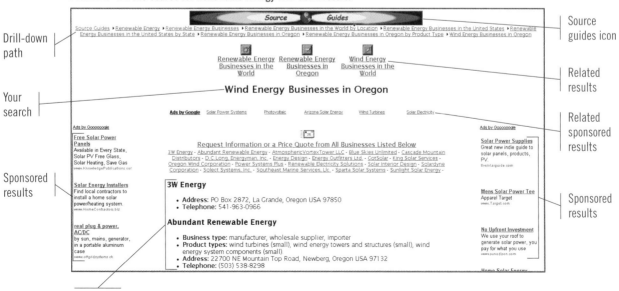

Understanding Evaluative Criteria

Evaluative criteria are standards used to determine if a Web site is appropriate for your needs. No matter what your subject or which search tool you use, resources you find must be evaluated. Web information can go directly from the author to you, with no intervening editorial or review process used for most printed material, requiring you to be more critical. In an earlier unit, you practiced evaluating search results to choose which pages to explore. After exploring sites that passed your search results evaluation, you will have eliminated some and kept others. Now the latter ones must pass through another level of assessment. Figure C-15 illustrates the criteria you should use in determining if a site is appropriate for your specific needs. Figure C-16 shows an example of identifying evaluative criteria on a Web page. ██████ You have found so many sites on your subject that you are concerned about being able to select the most appropriate ones to present to the team at the City Planning Office. Bob provides you with criteria to use to evaluate Web pages to determine which pages are appropriate for your needs.

DETAILS

Criteria include the following:

- **Organization**

  The way a Web site is organized is often almost as important as its content. Great content on a page can be defeated by poor design and functionality. Attractiveness and graphic features can mask a lack of meaningful content. Answer these questions as you evaluate a page:
  - Is the site well designed and functional? Is there a site map and Help page?
  - Is it easy to navigate? Do the navigational buttons and internal links work?
  - Is it searchable? Are there a variety of ways to access material?

QUICK TIP

If there is an e-mail link for the author or creator, feel free to write and ask questions about your research.

- **Authority**

  Knowing the author's name and qualifications is key to determining how credible or reliable the material is. Try a search for the author to see if he or she has written in the field. Consider these questions:
  - Is the author identified? Are the author's qualifications identified? Are resources documented?
  - Is there contact information for the author? Are other publications by the author listed?
  - Is the author associated with a university, a government agency, or an organization?

QUICK TIP

Is there a bibliography? Are resources well documented?

- **Objectivity and accuracy**

  A site's objectivity and accuracy greatly affects its appropriateness. Nothing is wrong with selling a product or advocating an idea, but that should be stated as the purpose of the page. You need to validate the site's objectivity and accuracy by looking at other online or printed information on the topic. Consider these questions:
  - Does the author state the purpose of the site? Is the content presented as fact or as opinion?
  - Is the publisher, sponsor, or host for the site identified?
  - What do other Web sites or articles say about the author or sponsor?

- **Scope**

  The **scope** of a site is the range of topics it covers. Consider these questions:
  - Is there an introduction or other information explaining the scope of the site?
  - Who is the intended audience? Is it useful for professionals? Lay people? Students?
  - Does the scope of the site match your needs?

QUICK TIP

You might need to go to the site's home page or About page to look for dates.

- **Currency**

  Currency or timeliness may or may not be an issue for your search. Consider these questions:
  - Is there a creation or revision date?
  - Are there many broken links? If so, this might indicate the site is not being updated or maintained.
  - Does the currency of the site match your needs?

FIGURE C-15: Evaluative criteria contributing to a site's appropriateness

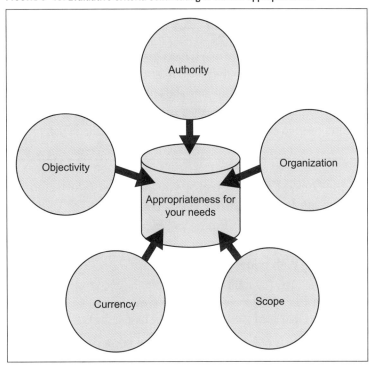

FIGURE C-16: Identifying evaluative criteria on a Web page (page from Florida Solar Energy Center)

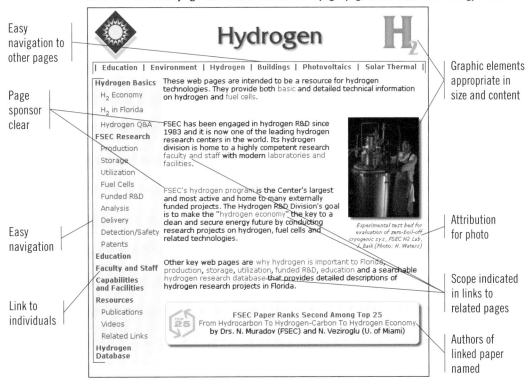

Clues to Use

Are there any objective Web pages?

No Web page is totally objective. Commercial sites (.com) usually exist to sell something. Nonprofit organizations (.org) usually have strong opinions about their causes. Even an educational page (.edu) can be affected by its creator's views. Ideally, these sites divulge their positions openly, but very often you have to dig around to find out. Educational (.edu) and government (.gov) sites generally are more objective, or at least support their ideas with documented facts. As long as you can ascertain a page's bias, you can come to your own conclusions about its content.

Internet Research

Evaluating a Web Page

Every time you use a search engine or a subject guide, you must choose which Web sites to include in your research. The evaluative criteria in the previous lesson are tools that enable you to quickly eliminate the least useful sites so that you can focus your time and energy on the most relevant ones. ⬛⬛⬛ You have located a site about renewable energy, which could be very useful to the city planning team. You think it might be appropriate but need to evaluate it more closely using the criteria Bob provided.

STEPS

TROUBLE

If a site has moved or disappeared from the Web, the Online Companion will link to a new site and provide new directions to follow.

1. **Go to the Online Companion at** www.course.com/illustrated/research3, **then click the DSIRE link (under "Specialized search engines")**

   The DSIRE (Database of State Incentives for Renewable Energy) home page opens, and should look similar to Figure C-17.

2. **Look over the Web page**

   As you scan the page, you realize the level of writing and its scope are appropriate. It provides a glossary, a searchable database, a library of reports and presentations, and more. You notice the About Us link and decide to follow it to learn something about the host of the site.

3. **Click the About Us link near the top of the page**

   You have now discovered that the sponsors of this site are IREC, an interstate council on renewable energy, the U.S. Department of Energy, and the North Carolina Solar Center, a program of the College of Engineering at North Carolina State University. You are satisfied that DSIRE is a reputable organization. You now want to check for contact information.

4. **Click the Contacts link**

   The Contacts page includes links to contact state energy officials, Department of Energy regional officials, and, most importantly, an e-mail address to contact DSIRE directly. There are also links near the top of the page to go to the home pages of the IREC and the North Carolina Solar Center (NCSC).

5. **Click the NC Solar Center link near the top of the page, click the Contact link near the top of the page, click the Click here to contact members of the Solar Center staff link, then click several names and look over the staff members' credentials**

6. **Choose one staffer's name, then record it in the Evaluating a Web Page table in your document**

   Now you want to go back to the DSIRE home page for any other information you can use to evaluate the site.

7. **Click your browser's Back button until you return to the DSIRE home page, then click the Links link**

   The links this site provides seem to be of high quality, as shown in Figure C-18. Now you want to check the timeliness of this page.

8. **Click your browser's Back button to return to the DSIRE home page, then look for the date the page was last updated**

9. **Record the date in the same table in your document, type your name at the top of your document, save, print, and close the document, then close your word-processing program**

FIGURE C-17: DSIRE home page

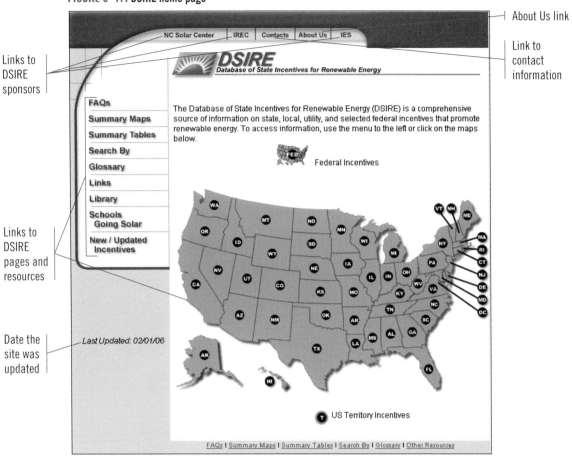

Links to DSIRE sponsors

About Us link

Link to contact information

Links to DSIRE pages and resources

Date the site was updated

FIGURE C-18: DSIRE's links to related resources

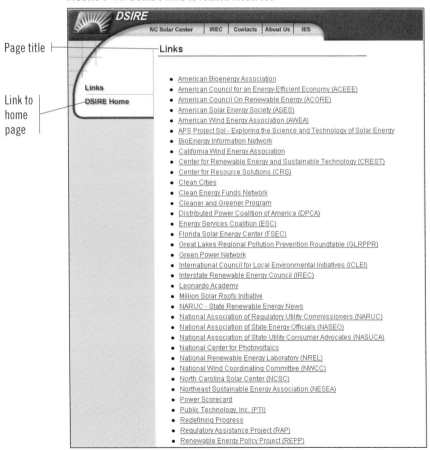

Page title

Link to home page

Internet Research

Practice

▼ CONCEPTS REVIEW

Label each of the parts in the subject guide shown in Figure C-19.

FIGURE C-1

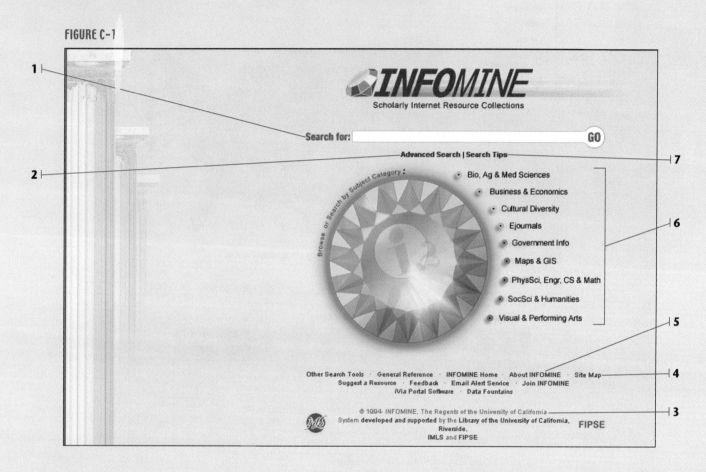

Match each term with the statement that best describes it.

8. **Scope**

9. **Hierarchy**

10. **Trailblazer pages**

11. **Annotation**

12. **Drill down**

13. **Dewey Decimal**

14. **Site map**

15. **Specialized search engine**

16. **Evaluative criteria**

17. **Distributed**

a. A carefully written summary or review

b. To click through topics to reach links on a results page

c. Standards that help you determine if a Web site is right for your needs

d. Often indexed in subject guides, these pages link to valuable sites, usually subject specific

e. A subject guide compiled by numerous editors and stored on numerous computers

f. Combines some of the best features of both a subject guide and a search engine

g. A stratified or ranked order

h. A subject classification system used by many libraries and some subject guides

i. An index to a Web site

j. The range of topics a site covers; it can be broad or narrow

Select the best answer from the list of choices.

18. **Traits that all subject guides share:**
    a. Are organized hierarchically and are selective in the Web sites they list.
    b. Are relatively small compared to search engines.
    c. Include annotations to the Web sites.
    d. All of the above

19. **One definition of *browsing* is:**
    a. Clicking through the hierarchy of topics at a subject guide.
    b. Using a local search engine to search a subject guide.
    c. Using criteria to evaluate a Web site.
    d. Finding out who wrote a Web page.

20. **A distributed subject guide:**
    a. Is maintained by one editor.
    b. Usually resides on only one computer.
    c. Is the same thing as a search engine.
    d. May lack standardization.

21. **An annotated subject guide:**
    a. Allows you to write reviews of Web sites.
    b. Contains reviews of Web sites.
    c. Reviews other subject guides.
    d. Allows you to search for reviews of search engines.

22. **A local search engine:**
    a. Is best searched with complex Boolean queries.
    b. Does not usually exist at a subject guide.
    c. Searches only in one city or state.
    d. Is best searched using one keyword or short phrase.

23. **Which is *not* a way subject guides are organized?**
    a. Alphabetically
    b. By hexadecimal
    c. By Dewey Decimal
    d. Topically

24. **Specialized search engines:**
    a. Only exist on a few topics.
    b. Are like a regular search engine except they index far more Web pages.
    c. Cannot be queried using Boolean operators.
    d. Share qualities of both subject guides and search engines.

25. **Which is a common way to find a specialized search engine?**
    a. Ask a librarian or professor.
    b. See if there is a link to one from a trailblazer page or a subject guide.
    c. Visit a collection of specialized search engines on the Web.
    d. All of the above.

26. **When evaluating a Web page to determine its authority, you should *not*:**
    a. Consider the qualifications of the author of a Web page.
    b. Consider the conviction with which an author writes.
    c. Look to see what else the author has written.
    d. Look to see if resources are well documented.

Internet Research

▼ SKILLS REVIEW

1. Understand subject guides.

a. Open the file IR C-2.doc from the drive and folder where your Data Files are located, save it as **Using Subject Guides** in the *YourName* folder where you are saving files for this book, then add your name at the top of the document.

b. Choose at least three of the five common traits of subject guides mentioned in Lesson 1.

c. In the Skill #1 table in your document, write a few sentences about how these traits make subject guides useful for Web research and different from search engines.

d. Save your document.

2. Browse a subject guide.

a. A friend is interested in changing careers and asks you to help her find information on companies offering good opportunities for a working mother.

b. Start your browser and go to the Online Companion at www.course.com/illustrated/research3.

c. Click the Librarians' Internet Index link under Subject guides.

d. Look over the general topics and click the Jobs link under Business.

e. In the resulting subtopics, click Women.

f. Look over these annotations and choose one that looks appropriate for this search.

g. In the Skill #2 table in your document, record the title of the Web site you chose, then save your document.

3. Search a subject guide.

a. You are writing a book and want to avoid plagiarizing the information you read.

b. Go to the Online Companion, then click the INFOMINE link.

c. In the Search text box, type **plagiarism**, then click Go.

d. In the Skill #3 table in your document, record how many Expert-selected Resources are listed.

e. Follow one link, choose a site, record the title in the same table, then save your document.

4. Navigate a subject guide.

a. Your younger brother is writing a report for his high school Social Studies class about families in Canada. He has one statistics book with some good information in it, but would like more. You notice the book has the Dewey number 310 on it. You decide to look in BUBL using the Dewey number for more information.

b. Go to the Online Companion, then click the BUBL LINK / 5:15 link.

c. Click 300 Social sciences.

d. On the next page, click 310 Collections of general statistics.

e. On the next page, click 317.3 Statistics of the United States and Canada.

f. In the Skill #4 table in your document, record the total number of Web sites listed under this link.

g. Look through the links and their annotations. Choose one that you think might be useful for your brother. Record its title, then save your document.

5. Tap trailblazer pages.

a. You are still keeping your eye open for online career material for your friend and have just run across The Occupational Outlook Handbook. You want to decide quickly if this is one that you want to share with her.

b. Go to the Online Companion, then click the Occupational Outlook Handbook link under "Specialized search engines."

c. Answer the questions posed in the Skill #5 table in your document, then save your document.

▼ SKILLS REVIEW (CONTINUED)

6. Use a specialized search engine.

a. You remember reading a great quote from Wayne Gretzky but can't quite recall how it was worded. It had something to do with the phrase "100% of your shots." You decide to try a specialty subject engine to find it.

b. Go to the Online Companion, then click the Quoteland.com link under "Specialized search engines."

c. Type **Gretzky** in the search form, then click Search.

d. Follow the link that Quoteland returns for Wayne Gretzky.

e. Look at the quotes on the results page, identify the one you are looking for, record the quote in the Skill #6 table in your document, then save your document.

7. Understand evaluative criteria.

a. In the Skill #7 table in your document, identify at least three criteria for evaluating Web pages for appropriateness.

b. In the same table, write a few sentences about each of the three criteria, including why the criteria is important and sample questions to answer to determine if the page meets the criteria.

c. Save your document.

8. Evaluate a Web page.

a. You are writing a paper on the history of mathematics. You found a Web page that might be relevant and want to evaluate it quickly.

b. Go to the Online Companion, then click the MacTutor History of Mathematics link under "Specialized search engines."

c. Answer the questions in the Skill #8 table in your document, then print, save, and close your document.

▼ INDEPENDENT CHALLENGE 1

Your company is thinking of designing new billboards and the graphic artist, who wants to use a retro look in one of her proposals, asks you to help her find examples of World War II poster art. You want to find something for her that you're sure is of good quality, so you turn to the INFOMINE subject guide.

a. Open the Online Companion at www.course.com/illustrated/research3, then click INFOMINE.

b. There are a couple of potential broad headings on the home page that might produce good results. Click the Government Info link.

c. When the search page opens, scroll to Browse Options if necessary, then click LCSH (for Library of Congress Subject Headings).

d. In the list of the alphabet, click the W link (for World War II), then click the appropriate letter range link for World War II.

e. Scroll down the alphabetical list until you find World War, 1939 – 1945 – Posters, then click the heading.

f. Start a new document in your word processor, then record the titles of the sites indexed.

g. Add your name to the document, then save it as **WWII Posters** in the *YourName* folder where you are saving files for this book.

Advanced Challenge Exercise

- Click the link for World War II Poster Database.
- Look over the site and identify ways to use it.
- At the bottom of your document, write about how you can search this site.
- Perform a search and identify a poster you find interesting, then display the full record to find out more about it.
- In your document, describe your search, and provide information about the poster you selected.

h. Add your name to your document, save it, print it, then close your document.

▼ INDEPENDENT CHALLENGE 2

You are beginning a new job working with a team of Web developers. You want to find some recommended sites on RSS before attending a meeting about setting up a feed.

    a. In your word processor, create a new document, add your name at the top, then save the document as **RSS** in the *YourName* folder where you are saving files for this book.

    b. Go to the Librarians' Internet Index, search RSS, then, in your document, record how many Web sites were listed in your results.

    c. Next in your document, record the order in which your results are listed/ranked.

    d. Choose one site and click the icon link to view more information. (*Hint:* The icon looks like a magnifying glass.)

    e. In your document, record the date this record was last modified by LII.

    f. Record the LII Topics under which this site is indexed.

    g. Click the topic RSS (Really Simple Syndication). Record the order in which these results are listed/ranked.

    h. Save, print, and close your document.

▼ INDEPENDENT CHALLENGE 3

The healthcare provider you work for has just posted a new Web page. The managers found the Web site shown in Figure C-20 and want you to evaluate it for them. Is it credible and good enough to include as a link on their Web page? They want you to present a list of reasons why it should or should not be included.

    a. Find this page on the Web.

    b. Evaluate the Web site by considering its organization, authority, scope, objectivity, and currency.

    c. In your word processor, start a new document, save it as **Web site evaluation** in the *YourName* folder where you are saving files for this book, then list your thoughts on why this site would or would not be an appropriate link on your employer's site.

    d. Include at least five reasons in your argument.

    e. Add your name to the document, then save, print, and close it.

FIGURE C-20

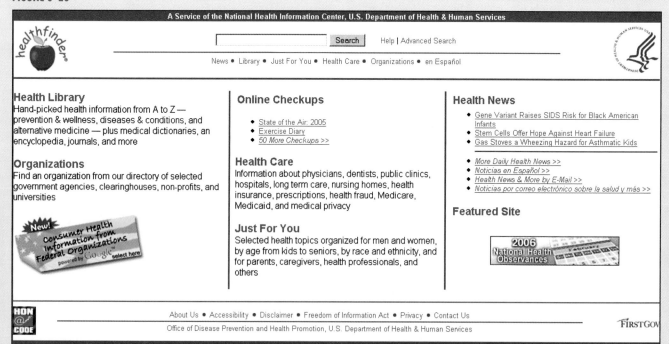

▼ INDEPENDENT CHALLENGE 4

You have a class assignment due for which you must use a credible Web site as one of your sources for a paper covering a topic of your choosing. You want to use a subject guide of academic quality to locate an appropriate site.

a. Go to a subject guide of your choice.

b. Find a few sources that you think might be useful for your chosen topic.

c. In your word processor, start a new document, save it as **My subject guide** in the *YourName* folder where you are saving files for this book, then describe which subject guide you used and how you searched (local search engine, drilling down, or another method).

d. How many sites did you find related to your topic?

e. Select one site that you think might be particularly relevant and evaluate it according to these criteria: organization, authority, scope, objectivity, and currency. Write at least one sentence about how the site meets each criterion.

f. Would you say this is an appropriate and credible Web site for your assignment?

g. Add your name to the document, save it, and print it.

Advanced Challenge Exercise

- You want to do another search to check for a site you might like better than the one you found in your last search, so you select a different subject guide.
- Find relevant sites.
- In a new document, describe which subject guide you used, how you searched (using a search form or drilling down), then record how many sites you found.
- Write a sentence about which subject guide was the most user friendly and which provided the single best result.

h. Save, print, and close your document, then exit your word-processing program.

During your exploration of subject guides, you found and printed the page shown in Figure C-21. Now you want to go back and quickly evaluate it before sharing it with a friend. Find and print the page, note at the top of the page whether you think it *is* or *is not* appropriate for use as a personal hockey resource, then write your name at the top of the printout.

FIGURE C-21

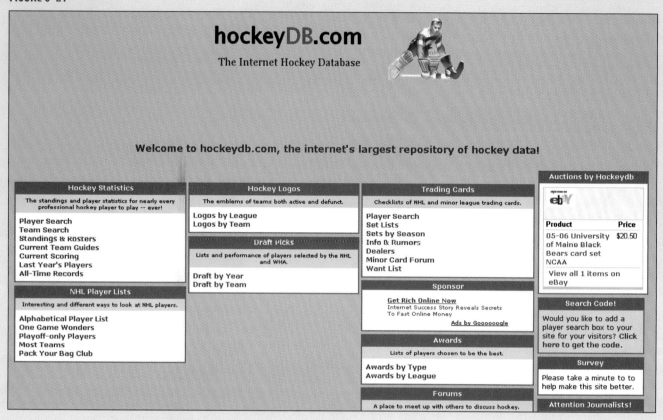

Finding Specialty Information

OBJECTIVES

Understand specialty information
Find people and places
Locate businesses
Search periodical databases
Find government information
Find online reference sources
Find mailing lists and newsgroups
Search with an intelligent agent

You have already learned to use search engines and subject guides for general research. However, sometimes the information you want is very specific, such as someone's name, the address of a business, or the definition of a word. This kind of specialty information is often stored in online databases that require direct access, making traditional search engines and most subject guides ineffective. Specialty information is accessed through specialty Web sites that include online telephone directories, maps, periodicals, government sites, mailing lists, and newsgroups. Until recently, you had to visit each of these specialty Web sites to retrieve information. Today, you can take advantage of intelligent search agents that automate this process by simultaneously retrieving information stored in many of these Web databases. You will be attending a conference in Washington, D.C., on renewable energy. In preparing for this conference, Bob suggests you continue your research on alternative energy using specialty Web sites and intelligent search agents.

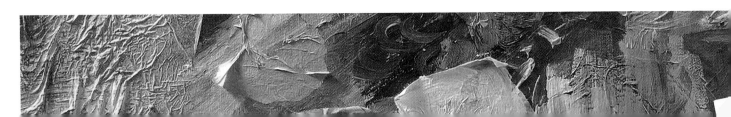

Understanding Specialty Information

By far, the largest part of the Internet is hidden from most search tools. This hidden content is called the **deep Web** or the **invisible Web**. The search engines you have used so far search for information on the **surface Web** or **visible Web**, which is the portion of the Web indexed by traditional search engine spiders. Deep Web content largely resides in online databases and is unavailable to traditional search engines and subject guides because these databases require direct queries at their sites. Common examples of databases are online phone books or newspaper and magazine archives. Other examples include **dynamically generated Web pages** that a database creates based on a specific query, or pages that require a login name and password. Pages that are not in HTML format, such as .pdf or .doc files, can also be difficult for search engine spiders to index. Figure D-1 provides a conceptual view of Internet content searched by traditional search engines and subject guides contrasted to the content searched by intelligent search agents and specialty search tools. ▓▓▓▓ Not wanting to ignore a large part of the information available via the Internet, you decide to learn about research tools that can help make the invisible Web usable. Bob provides some basics on using these specialty search tools.

DETAILS

The following are some important points to remember:

- **How to find specialty information**

  Typically, you locate hidden Web content by going to a specialty Web site and using its search form to query a database. Although the vast majority of the invisible Web is available publicly, some specialized databases require subscriptions. Because libraries pay the subscription fees for many of these specialty sites, such as the full-text magazine and newspaper article databases ProQuest, EBSCOhost, and InfoTrac, they are a good place to access these resources. You can also go to a "virtual library" such as the Internet Public Library (www.ipl.org), which links to these specialty Web sites from its reference section.

QUICK TIP

Be sure to read the About information at a specialty site before using it.

- **Scope and focus**

  By definition, specialty Web sites tend to have a narrower and deeper focus, usually resulting in higher-quality content. However, even two tools that focus on the same narrow area are not exactly alike. For example, various governmental agencies are charged with creating access to different, but sometimes overlapping, government information. The National Technical Information Service (NTIS) has a database of publications on scientific, technical, and business-related topics. The U.S. Census Bureau Web site primarily focuses on Web sites containing demographic information, but also features data related to business, as well as Census Bureau products, such as CD-ROMs and DVDs offered for sale. The Government Printing Office (GPO) is charged with making much of the information produced by the federal government accessible to citizens. State governments also usually provide their own searchable sites.

QUICK TIP

After registering with some "free" sites, you might see an increase in promotional e-mail, either from the site itself or from businesses to which they sold your address. This is the true price you pay for giving the site personal information. Always review the site's privacy information before sharing your address.

- **Free or pay?**

  Most specialty Web sites are either free or partially free. If they are commercial sites, they might give away some information but charge you for detailed data. Other sites might allow you free access, but require you to register with them—some require only an e-mail address or username and others require considerably more personal information. Some sites, including many newspaper sites, allow free access to their most recent files, but charge for access to archival files. If a site is going to charge you up front, it requires your credit card number—so don't give it out unless you want them to use it.

- **Incomplete coverage**

  Up-to-date, detailed information about people or businesses is hard to come by and, therefore, valuable. Companies guard proprietary information with security measures that prevent unauthorized access. So, although specialty Web sites provide access to much of the invisible Web, portions remain hidden.

- **Automatic searches**

  A newer breed of software called an **intelligent search agent** makes it possible to automatically retrieve information stored in multiple databases on the Web. An intelligent search agent can simultaneously query hundreds of databases (the deep Web) as well as traditional online resources (the surface Web). An intelligent search agent "knows" how to query each database, thus eliminating the need to visit individual sites and manually enter queries. However, you still need to manually search specialty databases that require fees or passwords.

FIGURE D-1: Internet content searched by traditional search engines and subject guides contrasted to that searched by intelligent search agents and specialty search tools*

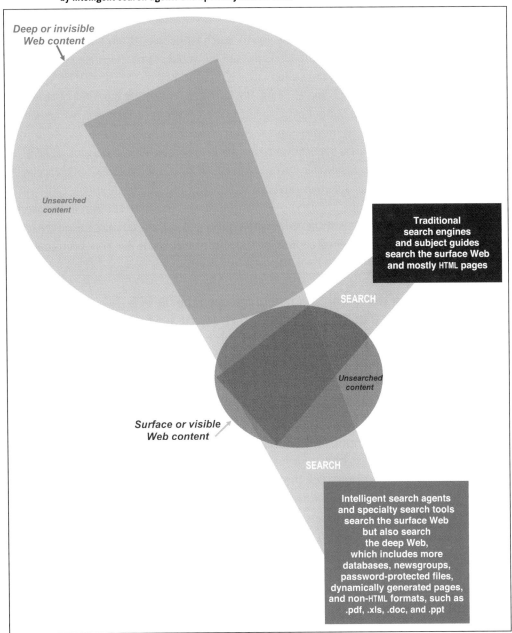

Deep or invisible Web content

Unsearched content

Traditional search engines and subject guides search the surface Web and mostly HTML pages

SEARCH

Unsearched content

Surface or visible Web content

SEARCH

Intelligent search agents and specialty search tools search the surface Web but also search the deep Web, which includes more databases, newsgroups, password-protected files, dynamically generated pages, and non-HTML formats, such as .pdf, .xls, .doc, and .ppt

* Conceptual only. If this figure were to scale, the deep Web portion would be hundreds of times larger than the surface Web portion.

Clues to Use

Visible and invisible Web

According to a white paper from Bright Planet (makers of DQM, an intelligent search agent), the invisible or deep Web is 500 times larger than the visible or surface Web (to see this white paper, click the The Deep Web link under "Deep Web" in the Online Companion). The visible or surface Web accounts for only about 13 billion pages. The deep Web contains approximately five trillion pages, largely hidden from the view of traditional search engines. Approximately 95% of the deep Web is available publicly (that is, it doesn't require a fee or password). For more information about the deep Web, click the links under "Deep Web" in the Online Companion.

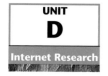

Finding People and Places

A variety of services on the Web allow you to search for people. At most of them, you can search for a person's phone number and street address just as you would search the white pages of a local phone book. Phone number and street address information is usually based on the information found in telephone books, which tend to be thorough and accurate. However, remember that they are not absolutely comprehensive because individuals can opt out of being listed. There is no centralized service that gathers e-mail information. Although some white pages sites search e-mail addresses, you should keep in mind that e-mail addresses tend to change frequently, making this kind of search less successful. ⬛⬛⬛ The Department of Energy Efficiency and Renewable Energy Network (EERE) is sponsoring a conference in Washington, D.C., for government officials interested in renewable energy. You plan to attend the conference. While you're on the East Coast, you hope to catch up with a relative who you think still lives in New York City. This relative just happens to share your name. When you explain to Bob that you want to find the relative's phone number, street address, and e-mail address, he suggests several online directories you could try.

STEPS

QUICK TIP
You do not need to use capital letters when searching names of people, cities, businesses, and so on.

1. **Start your word-processing program, open the file** IR D-1.doc **from the drive and folder where your Data Files are located, then save it as** Specialty Information **in the** *YourName* **folder where you are saving files for this book**
   You will use this file to record information you find in your searches.

2. **Start your browser, go to the Online Companion at** www.course.com/ illustrated/research3, **then click the** Yahoo! People Search link **(under "White Pages")**
   The Yahoo! People Search home page opens, as shown in Figure D-2.

TROUBLE
If there are no results, click the Try your search again link and leave the First Name text box empty or enter another name.

3. **Under the US Phone and Address Search heading, type your** first initial **in the First Name/Initial text box, your** last name **in the Last Name text box,** New York **in the City/Town text box, click the** State drop-down list box, **scroll down and click** New York, **then click** Phone and Address Search
   A list of names should appear, as shown in Figure D-3. Directory searches often provide better results using just an initial, rather than a first name. Notice there are sponsored results and advertisement links for advanced searches requiring you to pay a fee, which is often substantial, by using your credit card online. Notice also your search is shown near the top of the screen, where you can make changes to the search. Near the bottom of the screen is the option to search the Web. If your results include a Map link, you can click this for directions.

4. **Choose one name and phone number, then record it in** Finding People and Places table **in your document**

QUICK TIP
If there are no results, try your search again and leave the First Name/Initial text box empty or enter another name.

5. **Click the** name **in the browser window (it should be underlined on your screen)**
   A separate page opens with your person's personal data. You decide to see if you can find an e-mail address.

6. **Click your browser's** Back button **twice to return to the Yahoo People Search page**

7. **Beneath the Email Search heading, type your** first initial **in the First Name/Initial text box, type your** last name **in the Last Name text box, then click** Email Search
   A list of names should appear, as shown in Figure D-4.

QUICK TIP
There are other e-mail directory services listed in the Online Companion.

8. **Scroll through the results list, select a name, use the** Finding People and Places table **to enter the name and e-mail address of the person, then save the document**
   The name you select might have a little or a lot of information, depending on how much information the person provided.

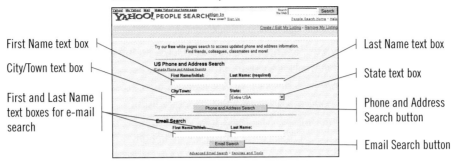

FIGURE D-2: Yahoo! People Search form

First Name text box

City/Town text box

First and Last Name text boxes for e-mail search

Last Name text box

State text box

Phone and Address Search button

Email Search button

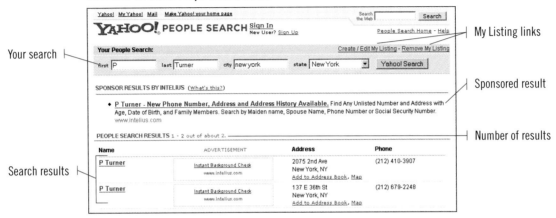

FIGURE D-3: Yahoo! People Search results

Your search

Search results

My Listing links

Sponsored result

Number of results

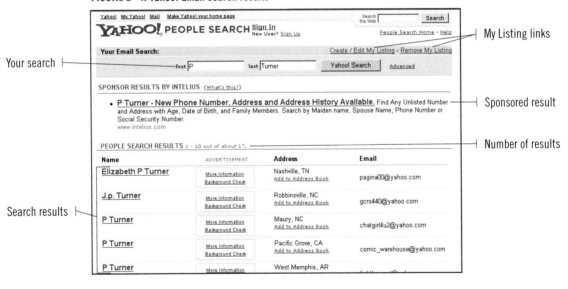

FIGURE D-4: Yahoo! Email Search results

Your search

Search results

My Listing links

Sponsored result

Number of results

Clues to Use

Finding places

Before the World Wide Web, you had to buy a map or go to the library to find out how to get where you wanted to go. Now the Web offers quite a few good map and locator Web sites. Many of these sites also provide trip planners and driving directions. In addition, they provide links to hotels, historical sites, and other attractions along the way. The "Other resources" section of the Online Companion provides links to map sites with driving directions for the United States, such as Maps On Us and Yahoo! Maps. Yahoo! and Google also cover Canada. MapQuest has sites specific to many countries, including the UK (www.mapquest.co.uk), Germany (www.mapquest.de), and France (www.mapquest.fr).

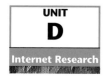

Locating Businesses

Just as there are many sites for finding people and places on the Web, there are also many yellow pages sites for finding businesses in the United States and worldwide, as shown in Table D-1. The site AnyWho (listed in the Online Companion) provides a list of international directories. The most high-powered business finders, such as Switchboard.com, integrate business directory listings with maps and travel planners. Most of the yellow pages directories on the Web build their databases from accurate and up-to-date information and allow new businesses to add their own information at any time. There is no charge to a business for the basic address and telephone listings. However, if a business wants to include a link to its Web site or an advertisement, it is charged for the service. ▨▨▨ While you are in Washington, D.C., you hope to meet with an expert in wind energy legislation. You need directions to her office. You remember that the name of the organization is something like "Wind Energy," and it's either in Washington, D.C., or Arlington, Virginia. Bob suggests using Switchboard.com.

STEPS

QUICK TIP

In a directory database such as Switchboard, *not* entering all your data at once is often the best search strategy.

1. **Go to the Online Companion at** www.course.com/illustrated/research3, **then click the Switchboard link (under "Yellow Pages")**
   The Switchboard Web site appears. You can use this Web site to find a person, a business, or a product.

2. **Make sure the Find a Business option button is selected, then click the Advanced search link**
   The Switchboard Find a Business advanced search form appears, as shown in Figure D-5.

3. **Click the Search Near a Location option button if necessary, click in the And / Or Search by Business Name text box and type wind energy, click in the City text box and type arlington, click in the St text box and type va, then click SEARCH**
   Figure D-6 illustrates your results. You see that the office for which you were looking, American Wind Energy, is listed as being on C Street NW in Washington, D.C. Now you'd like to see a map.

4. **Click the Map link under the listing for American Wind Energy**
   You note the location and, because you'll be in the area at lunchtime, decide to see what restaurants are nearby.

5. **Click your browser's Back button to return to the listing, click the What's Nearby? link, scroll if necessary, click the Restaurants link under Food & Dining, then click the Restaurants-Pizza link**
   The search results appear, as shown in Figure D-7. Note that there might be a link to the restaurant's Web site and that you can send the listing to your mobile phone.

6. **Choose a pizzeria from the list that appears, record the name and address in the Locating Businesses table in your document, then save the document**

TABLE D-1: Features of business finder Web sites (see the Online Companion)

name	country	people	business	toll-free numbers	maps	city pages
AnyWho	USA	X	X	X	X	
Canada411	Canada	X	X			
Europages	Europe		X			
Scoot	UK, France, Belgium, Netherlands		X			
SuperPages	USA	X	X		X	X
Switchboard	USA	X	X		X	X
UKphonebook	UK	X				
Yell.com	UK		X			
Yellowpages.ca	Canada	X	X	X		X
Yellowpages.com.au	Australia	X	X		X	

FIGURE D-5: Switchboard's Find a Business advanced search form

Find a Business advanced search form

Option to search IN or NEAR a location

Category/Keyword text box

And/Or Business Name text box

City text box

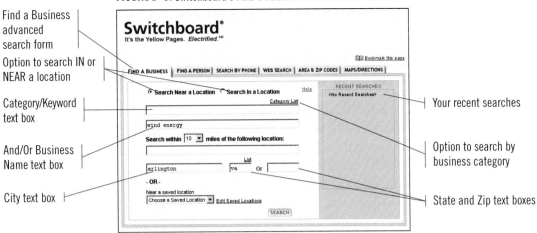

Your recent searches

Option to search by business category

State and Zip text boxes

FIGURE D-6: Switchboard search *wind energy near Arlington, VA*

Search results

Options for further information

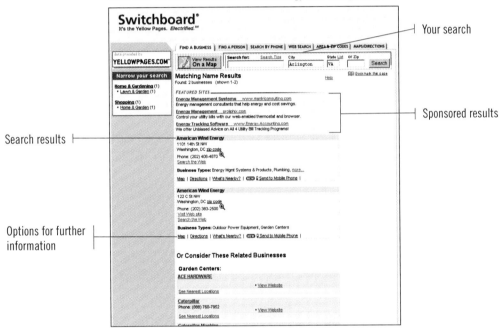

Your search

Sponsored results

FIGURE D-7: Switchboard search for pizzerias near your meeting in Arlington, VA

Search results

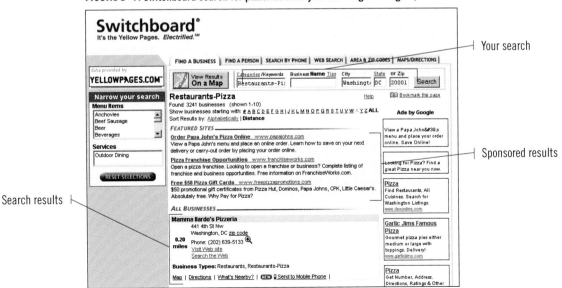

Your search

Sponsored results

Searching Periodical Databases

Some of the most authoritative and current information hidden in the invisible Web is stored in **periodical databases**. These include the archives of popular magazines, newspapers, and scholarly journals. Table D-2 describes the differences between different types of periodicals and gives an example of each type. Some periodicals, such as *Salon* or *First Monday*, exist only in electronic format on the Web. Other periodicals, such as *The Times* or *The New York Times*, have an online version that might not carry all the same stories as the printed version and might include some stories not seen in print. In addition, subscription databases such as ProQuest and InfoTrac, available at libraries, store electronic versions of thousands of periodical titles. Most online periodical databases provide limited recent information for free, but require registration or payment for older materials. ▧▧▧▧ Before leaving for the conference in Washington, D.C., you decide to look for some current articles on alternative energy topics to read on the plane. Bob provides a list of potential databases and you decide to begin with *The Times* of London.

STEPS

QUICK TIP

When you use *The New York Times*, or other individual periodical indexes, you may encounter some articles that are available to subscribers only. However, your librarian can usually get these articles for you.

TROUBLE

If your search did not find any articles, try another search using another alternative energy topic. If your search still does not yield any articles, enter any other keywords.

1. **Go to the Online Companion at** www.course.com/illustrated/research3, **then click** The Times link **(under "Periodical listings")**

   The TimesOnline home page opens.

2. **Type** "renewable energy" **in the Search text box, then click** Go

   A new TimesOnline window opens listing your search results with links to relevant articles. The percentage figure beside each title indicates its relevance to your search.

3. **Scroll the results page**

   In the Search Tips section, notice that you are searching only the last seven days of content and that you are advised to capitalize proper nouns. Also note that if you want an older article, you must subscribe and pay a fee.

4. **Click the** title **of an article that you think might be interesting, read it, then record the article title in the** Searching Periodical Databases table **in your document**

   Next, you want to try searching a periodical database that indexes multiple titles.

5. **Go to the Online Companion, then click the** MagPortal.com link **(under "Periodical listings")**

   MagPortal offers broad topical categories you can navigate by drilling down to find articles of interest. For example, Figure D-8 shows results from choosing the broad category Science & Technology, and then choosing a category within it, Environment & Geology. The site also offers a Search text box to use for searching with keywords.

6. **Type** "renewable energy" **in the Search text box, then click** Search

   A list of online articles with brief annotations appears, as shown in Figure D-9. The small wavy line icon at the end of each article links you to similar articles.

7. **Click the** title **of one of the articles**

   You should be taken from the MagPortal Web site to the publication site.

8. **Record the article title in the same table in your document, then save your document**

FIGURE D-8: Browsing MagPortal via subject categories

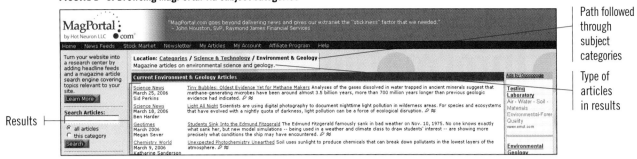

Path followed through subject categories

Type of articles in results

Results

FIGURE D-9: MagPortal search "renewable energy"

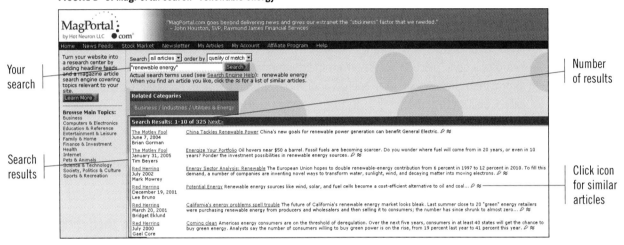

Your search

Search results

Number of results

Click icon for similar articles

TABLE D-2: Periodicals and their distinguishing characteristics

periodical type	purpose	publisher	audience	documentation	example
Scholarly/research	Original research/ experiments	University/ organization	Scholars/ professionals/ university students	Citations/ bibliography	*Harvard Education Review*
Professional/ special interest	Professional practice/ case studies	Organization	Professionals/ university students	May cite or provide bibliography	*Journal of Accountancy*
General interest	Inform/entertain/ advocate	Commercial	Knowledgeable reader/possibly technical	May mention sources	*The New York Times*
Popular	Entertain	Commercial	General audience/ simple language	Rarely mentions sources	*Metropolitan Home*

Clues to Use

Where to find online periodicals

Some sites on the Web are "online newsstands." They collect links to electronic periodicals from around the world on all topics. Examples are provided in the Online Companion. They include the ipl (Internet Public Library) Online Serials collection, the Librarians' Internet Index Magazine Topics, and NewsDirectory.com. Other sites such as MagPortal.com and FindArticles allow you to search many online magazine databases simultaneously. The most comprehensive online databases, such as ProQuest and InfoTrac, are available through public, school, and academic libraries. As long as you are affiliated with a library, you can access these databases from home at no charge—just ask your local librarian for guidance.

Finding Government Information

Governments are prodigious producers and users of information. Large gateways, called **portals**, create access to different segments of government information, as shown in Table D-3. Portals originated in the commercial sector, with such sites as America Online and MSN that offered their version of "everything"— search engines, news, shopping, e-mail, chat, and more. They each endeavored to create an attractive and useful site so that you would never go anywhere else to find information. The idea of a portal caught on and now many other sites have carved out niches in various subject areas, especially in industry and government. These portals, which are limited by subject, are also referred to as **vortals**, or vertical portals. Government portals provide access to online information or to printed materials that you can purchase from government agencies or borrow from libraries. ⬛⬛⬛ While attending the EERE conference in Washington, D.C., you heard of a good place to access government information online—FirstGov. You want to see if you can find information there about solar energy and, more specifically, about a project discussed at the conference, called "million solar roofs."

STEPS

QUICK TIP

Make sure the Specialty Information document is still open in your word processor.

1. **Go to the Online Companion at** www.course.com/illustrated/research3, **then click the** FirstGov link **(under "Government references")**
   The FirstGov Web site opens.

2. **Type** "solar energy" **in the Search Government Websites text box, then click** Search
   A list of search results opens, as shown in Figure D-10.

3. **Scroll through the results, choose one site, then record its URL in the** Finding Government Information table **in the Specialty Information document**

4. **Click the** Advanced Search link
   The FirstGov Advanced Search form opens.

5. **Clear the search form, if necessary, type** million solar roofs **in the This exact phrase text box, then press** [Enter] **to initiate the search**
   Now you want to limit this search so that all the results must include Oregon.

6. **Click the** Advanced Search **link, click the** Search in **list box, scroll down and click** Oregon, **then press** [Enter] **to initiate the search**
   Your search results open, as shown in Figure D-11. Note that, although the box showing your search at the top of the page does not mention that the search limited results to those in Oregon, many of the results contain the word "Oregon."

7. **Choose one site from your results, record the URL in the same table in your document, then save the document**

FIGURE D-10: FirstGov search "solar energy"

Your search

Search results

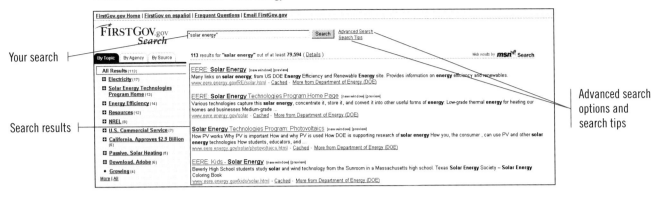

Advanced search options and search tips

FIGURE D-11: FirstGov search "million solar roofs" Oregon

Your search

Search results

You limited your search to results in Oregon; although this is not reflected in the search statement above, you can see from the results that the search was performed correctly

TABLE D-3: Specialized government portals (see Online Companion)

name	features
Australian Commonwealth Government Information	Australian federal and state information
Canadian Government Information on the Internet	Canadian federal, provincial, and municipal information
FedWorld (US)	Sponsored by the National Technical Information Service (NTIS) Covers scientific, technical, and engineering information Some links to government Web sites Most links to reports and publications available for purchase
FirstGov (US)	Most comprehensive site for U.S. government information online Links to over 20,000 federal and state government Web sites
DirectGov	Central and local government information for the United Kingdom
U.S. Government Printing Office	Links to federal publications Provides catalog of government documents available for purchase Catalog of libraries that own specific documents
University of Michigan Documents Center	Most complete guide to government information Links to local, state, national, and international government sites

Finding Online Reference Sources

Online reference sources are similar to their counterparts on library shelves. They include almanacs, dictionaries, directories, and encyclopedias—the kinds of resources you don't read cover to cover, but refer to often. Library Web sites almost always link to a variety of online reference sources, some of them licensed exclusively for their patrons' use. There are also virtual libraries, such as ipl, The Internet Public Library, that exist solely to bring together valuable Web sites and reference tools. ▰▰▰▰ You have returned from the EERE conference and are ready to finish your final list of alternative energy Web resources, but would like to find a few reliable online reference resources. Bob suggests looking through the reference sources at ipl.

STEPS

QUICK TIP

It's a good idea, when you find good reference sites, to add them to your browser's Favorites or Bookmarks file for easy access.

1. **Go to the Online Companion at** www.course.com/illustrated/research3, **click the** ipl Reference Page link **(under "Online references"), then click** Subject Collections
   The Internet Public Library main subject categories page appears. You want to look over the reference sources indexed here.

2. **Click** Reference, **click** Census Data & Demographics, **scroll down, then click** Statistical Resources on the Web
   This link takes you to the University of Michigan Documents Center Web page. You notice this reference tool links to statistical information in multiple categories. You decide to return to the ipl site and view the Energy subject category.

3. **Click your browser's** Back button **to return to the Census Data and Demographics links at ipl, scroll up to the top of the page, then point to the** Science & Tech link **under Subject Collections on the left side of your screen**
   A cascading menu of subtopics opens.

4. **Click** Energy **in the Science & Tech cascading menu, browse the resources, choose one link that seems helpful for your project, then record the URL in the** Finding Online Reference Sources table **in the Specialty Information document**
   Figure D-12 shows the ipl Energy reference resources page. You scan the page and notice a link to KidSpace in the list of links on the left side of your screen. You decide to see if there is an alternative energy site for children that you might want to include.

5. **Click** KidSpace **in the Subject Collections list, type** renewable energy **in the Search text box, click** Search, **and then click the** View all results in Kidspace **link**
   The search form for KidSpace is shown in Figure D-13.

6. **Choose a page to include in your report, then record the URL in the same table in your document**
   You want to see more links to online reference resources.

7. **Click your browser's** Back button **to return to the Online Companion, click the** Librarians' Internet Index link **(under "Subject Guides"), click the** Reference link, **click the** Statistics link, **click the** Power Resources link, **choose one URL, record the URL in the same table in your document, then save the document**

FIGURE D-12: ipl energy reference sources

Path showing where you are as you drill down into subject categories

Subject categories that open menus to subtopics

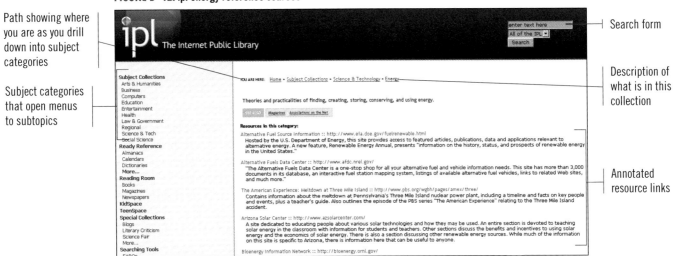

Search form

Description of what is in this collection

Annotated resource links

FIGURE D-13: ipl's KidSpace search form

KidSpace search form

Links to annotated reference resources appropriate for children

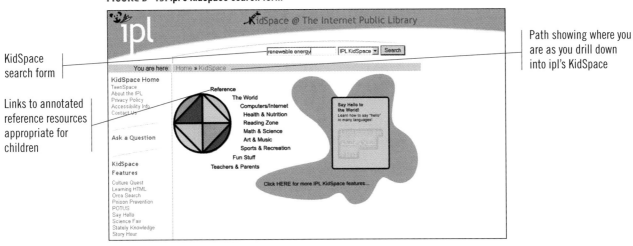

Path showing where you are as you drill down into ipl's KidSpace

Clues to Use

Online reference sources about the Internet

The Web includes reference sources on just about any topic. If you are working on a special research topic, you can always find good sources at the Reference sections of the Internet Public Library or the Librarians' Internet Index and add them temporarily to your browser's Bookmark or Favorite files. For instance, if you were studying the Internet, the following might be good sources to have close at hand:

name	resource type	features
FILExt	Dictionary	Lists most Internet file extensions; defines extensions and links to more information
Netiquette Home Page	Book	Provides the basics of Netiquette, at work and at home; covers primarily e-mail and newsgroups
Webopedia	Dictionary/encyclopedia	Covers computer and Internet terminology; provides paragraph definitions and links
Living Internet	Encyclopedia	Covers the Internet, the Web, e-mail, chat, newsgroups, and mailing lists; articles include history and how-to information
Internet Tutorials (Univ. of Albany Libraries)	Tutorial	Covers Using the Web, Searching the Web, Browsers, and Training; provides links and how-to tips
LII.org (Internet Guides and Search Tools Page)	Subject guide	Provides reliable links to answer almost any Internet question; covers searching, Web design, history, law, children, and more

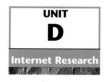

Finding Mailing Lists and Newsgroups

The Internet provides a variety of ways to communicate and interact with other people. On the Web, you can instantly become part of discussions of current issues and breaking news by subscribing to a **mailing list**, which allows you to e-mail messages to all other members of the list automatically. Mailing lists are often called **listservs** after the software that supports them. Another major method of information exchange on the Internet is **newsgroups**, virtual bulletin boards where messages on thousands of topics are posted daily. Newsgroups are often referred to collectively as **Usenet** after the system that distributes them. Anyone on the Internet can read and respond to the postings in a newsgroup, though you might be required to register. As the posted topics diverge, they are broken off into different **threads**, or subtopics. By searching the archives of discussion postings, you can also tap into primary documents that follow the development of topics from many personal and unconventional angles. You can find links to mailing lists and newsgroups about specific subjects on trailblazer Web pages, or you can search specific sites that list mailing lists or newsgroups. ▓▓▓▓ The EERE conference in Washington, D.C., was a great opportunity to meet people interested in alternative energy sources. Bob suggests you continue to communicate with other people who are interested in alternative energy topics through discussion groups. You remember seeing energy-related discussion groups when searching EERE's site, so you decide to start there.

STEPS

1. **Go to the Online Companion at** www.course.com/illustrated/research3, **click the** EERE link **(under "Subject guides"), click the** Biomass link **under Renewable Energy, then click** Discussion Groups **under Biomass Organizations & Resources**

   A page of links to newsgroups and mailing lists opens, as shown in Figure D-14.

   > **QUICK TIP**
   > Subscription addresses are in the following format: *listname-subscribe@ someplace.org.*

2. **Click the** Alternative Energy mailing list link, **find the** subscription address, **record it in the** Finding Mailing Lists and Newsgroups table **in your document, save and close the document, then exit the word-processing program**

3. **Go to the Online Companion, click the** Google link **(under "Search engines"), then click the** Groups tab **above the Google Search text box**

   Google includes a Search Groups text box, where you can search the archives of Usenet postings with keywords.

4. **Click the** Science and Technology link

   A collection of subgroups appears, with a complete list of newsgroups beneath the subgroups. To narrow the search, you decide to use Google's Directory Search.

5. **In the Directory Search text box, type** "alternative energy" **and then click** Directory Search

   A more restricted collection of subgroups and newsgroups appears. Newsgroup names are hierarchical and mnemonic. For example, a scientific group that discusses energy might be called sci.energy. Different parts of the name are separated by periods.

   > **QUICK TIP**
   > To participate in any of the threads at sci.energy, click "Post a new message to sci.energy." However, first you would need to register and obtain a password.

6. **Scroll through the newsgroups list in the lower part of the page, then click the** sci.energy link

   A list of postings to the sci.energy newsgroup appears, as shown in Figure D-15. This is the archive of the various newsgroup threads.

7. **Scroll down the page, find a thread of interest to you, print one page of the postings, then write your name at the top of the page**

   You are interested in reading more about the uses and development of Usenet Newsgroups.

8. **Go to the Online Companion, click the** Development of Usenet link **(under "Online references"), then read the article titled "The Social Forces Behind the Development of Usenet"**

FIGURE D-14: EERE's Biomass discussion groups

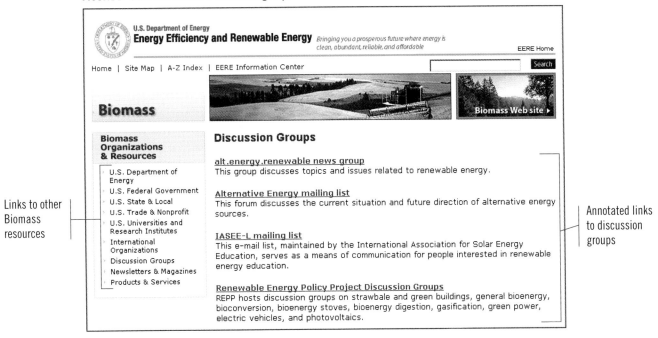

Links to other Biomass resources

Annotated links to discussion groups

FIGURE D-15: Google newsgroup directory for sci.energy

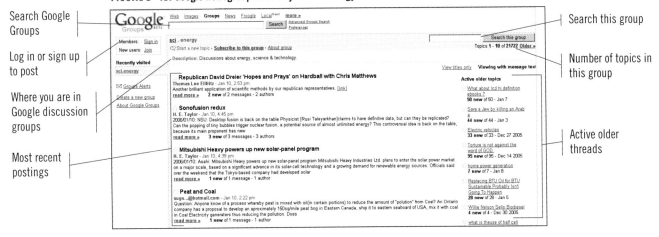

Search Google Groups

Log in or sign up to post

Where you are in Google discussion groups

Most recent postings

Search this group

Number of topics in this group

Active older threads

Clues to Use

Netiquette

Netiquette is the word Internet users use to describe the protocol and common rules of courtesy used by people on the Internet. For example, when you use a mailing list, you need to know that there are two separate e-mail addresses that have very different functions. You use the subscription address (also known as administrative address) to send messages asking the administrator to add or drop your name from the list. The list address is the place to send your actual list correspondence. If you use the wrong address and send your subscription information to the 10,000 or more members of a list, more than one might e-mail you and politely let you know that

you should use the *other* address. (If any member e-mails you and *impolitely* tells you so, this is called a "flame.")

Before you post to a newsgroup, it is good form to read the FAQs (frequently asked questions) and some of the more recent postings. In this way, you will ensure that you don't post a message to an inappropriate group, or ask a question that has been answered in a recent thread. For more information on netiquette, click the Netiquette Home Page link under "Online references" in the Online Companion.

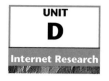

Searching with an Intelligent Agent

As the Internet grows and becomes more diverse, finding the correct information is more of a challenge. Fortunately, tools are evolving that make searching the visible and invisible parts of the Web simpler and more comprehensive. An **intelligent search agent**, or search bot, is a software program that automates search activities that traditional search services aren't programmed to perform, such as searching through online databases. One of the most powerful of the freely available intelligent search agents is IncyWincy, which can simultaneously query multiple databases, specialty search engines, and subject guides. IncyWincy "knows" how to query each database, eliminating the need to visit individual sites and manually enter queries. In addition, IncyWincy scores search results based on the relevancy to your query, making it faster and easier to find the information you need. ▰▰▰▰▰ You want to locate the latest business information about alternative energy, and decide to try using an intelligent agent to search more efficiently and effectively.

STEPS

1. **Go to the Online Companion at** www.course.com/illustrated/research3, **then click the** IncyWincy link **(under "Intelligent Search Agents")**

   The IncyWincy Web site opens. The Search text box at the top of the page queries multiple search engines simultaneously. Table D-4 describes the search options listed to the right of the Search text box.

2. **Click the** Preferences link

   The Preferences option provides the means to narrow your search and, hence, improve the relevancy of your search results. A page opens with a list of Categories from which you can choose a subject area. Each Category links to a collection of related Subcategories, which let you further target your search. Because you are looking for business information about alternative energy, you decide to use the Business Category.

   > **TROUBLE**
   > Depending on the cookies on your machine, you may see a link to "Preferences" or you may see a link to "Preference Boost;" both are correct.

3. **Under the "Select Categories" heading, click the** Business link

   A set of Subcategories of Business is listed, as shown in Figure D-16. Notice that the Business Category link now appears in black, indicating it has been selected. To limit your search further, you decide to examine and choose the most relevant subcategory of business.

   > **QUICK TIP**
   > To search all the Subcategories for the Business Category, click the All of Business check box.

4. **Scroll down the Subcategories of Business list, then click the** Energy and Environment check box

   A check mark appears in front of the chosen Subcategory and the page reloads. You are now ready to enter your complex query and have IncyWincy search the chosen resources.

   > **QUICK TIP**
   > To quickly remove all previously selected search Categories and associated Subcategories, click the Delete all categories link.

5. **In the Search text box, type** "alternative energy" OR "renewable energy", **then click** Search

   A page with the first search results opens, as shown in Figure D-17. The Web Pages heading displays the total number of search results. Each search result typically includes a page title, summary, URL, relevancy score, and date. For easy identification, keywords and phrases from your search query appear bolded in the search results.

6. **Click the page title of a result that interests you, read the information, then use your browser's** Back button **to return to the IncyWincy search results page**

7. **Use your browser's** Print button **to print the page, write your name at the top of the printout, then close the Web browser**

FIGURE D-16: IncyWincy Business Subcategories

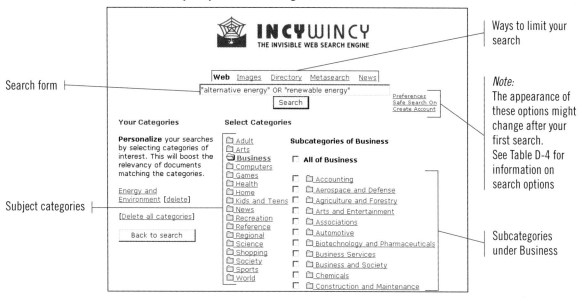

Search form

Subject categories

Ways to limit your search

Note:
The appearance of these options might change after your first search.
See Table D-4 for information on search options

Subcategories under Business

FIGURE D-17: IncyWincy search "renewable energy" OR "alternative energy"

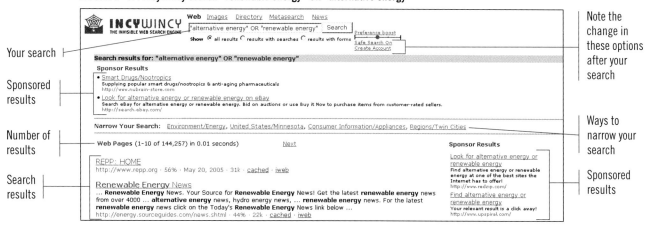

Your search

Sponsored results

Number of results

Search results

Note the change in these options after your search

Ways to narrow your search

Sponsored results

TABLE D-4: Search options for IncyWincy

option	description
Advanced Search/ Basic Search	Basic Search is the default search form; Advanced Search is a complex search form, which lets you specify the following: • *Scope* of a search controls whether just Web pages are shown in search results or search forms are displayed as well • *Query Operator* selects a Boolean operator to use in a search query (e.g., AND, OR, exact phrase) • *Number of Search Results* controls how many search results are displayed per page (default is 10) • *Duplicate Filter* removes identical documents from search results • *Number of Related Search Engines* indicates how many similar search engines are queried at one time (default is six) • *Auto Search* causes IncyWincy to automatically perform search queries • *Number of Search Results per Search Engine* controls the number of results accepted from each engine
Preference Boost	Provides search Categories and Subcategories to narrow a search and improve results
Safe Search Off/On	Safe Search On filters out adult content; Safe Search Off allows all content in search results
Create Account	Allows you to register for free and create a Basic Account, which provides the following: • *Alert* automatically tracks search results and notifies you when new information on a query becomes available • *Customized Page* lets you generate tailored search pages and news pages with your selection of sources • *Mail Account* provides 50 KB of mail space to organize alerts and to share your research results with others

Practice

▼ CONCEPTS REVIEW

Label each of the elements of the following Google Groups archive page.

FIGURE D-18

Match each term with the statement that best describes it.

8. Visible Web
9. Dynamic Web page
10. White pages
11. Yellow pages
12. Internet Public Library
13. Portal
14. Mailing list
15. Newsgroup
16. Intelligent search agent

a. Web sites with "people finder" tools
b. An example of a virtual library
c. A gateway to large segments of related Web information
d. An Internet bulletin board
e. A software program that automates search activities
f. Allows you to send and receive e-mail to and from a group of subscribers
g. The portion of the Web accessible to search engine indexing programs
h. Web sites that help you find businesses
i. A Web page that is generated when you request it

Select the best answer from the list of choices.

17. The invisible Web:
    a. Is not accessible.
    b. Consists mostly of pages written in HTML.
    c. Is much smaller than the visible Web.
    d. Is also known as the deep Web.

18. **You would not usually access specialty research tools by:**
    a. Asking a librarian.
    b. Using a search engine.
    c. Using a library's Web site.
    d. Using a virtual library site.

19. **Specialty sites might:**
    a. Require you to pay for the service.
    b. Allow you a few free searches and ask you to pay for more.
    c. Give away some information but charge for some too.
    d. All of the above

20. **One reason that online coverage can be incomplete is:**
    a. Companies like to give out proprietary information.
    b. Copyright law allows anyone to put current editions online.
    c. Many people value their privacy.
    d. New information has little value in today's marketplace.

21. **You would usually look for _____ at an online White Pages site.**
    a. A person's address
    b. A person's e-mail address
    c. A person's phone number
    d. All of the above

22. **A good place to search for information about businesses in the UK and France is:**
    a. The Librarians' Internet Index.
    b. Scoot.
    c. Yellowpages.ca.
    d. Switchboard.

23. **The subtopics that appear within a newsgroup are called:**
    a. Threads.
    b. Mailing lists.
    c. Listservs.
    d. Usenets.

24. **A site that links to local, state, federal, foreign, and multinational government links is:**
    a. FirstGov.
    b. University of Michigan Documents Center.
    c. FedWorld.
    d. United States Government Printing Office.

25. **IncyWincy is an example of:**
    a. A search engine.
    b. A subject guide.
    c. An intelligent search agent.
    d. A Yellow Pages site.

26. **When using IncyWincy, you select the categories to search by clicking:**
   a. A vertical search group.
   b. The Directory link.
   c. The Preferences link.
   d. b and c

▼ SKILLS REVIEW

1. **Understand specialty information.**
   a. Start your word-processing program, open the file IR D-2.doc from the drive and folder where your Data Files are located, then save it as **Specialty Searches** in the *YourName* folder where you are saving files for this book.
   b. Use the Skill #1 table in your document to write a sentence defining the invisible Web or deep Web.
   c. In the same table, list three sources that search the deep Web.

2. **Find people and places.**
   a. Go to the Online Companion at www.course.com/illustrated/research3, then click the 411Locate link under "White Pages."
   b. In the White Pages Search form, type your first and last name (or a friend's name) into the appropriate text boxes.
   c. Click Find.
   d. Click your name (or your friend's name) on the results page. If there are no unsponsored results, try a different name.
   e. Print the resulting page of information, then write your name at the top of the page.

3. **Locate businesses.**
   a. In the Online Companion, click the Switchboard site under "Yellow Pages," then click Find a Business.
   b. Type a Type of Business (or a Business Name), a City, and a State, then click Search.
   c. Click an appropriate business category on the resulting page. (If there are no resulting businesses, go back and choose another type of business.)
   d. Scroll down the results page and find a business located in the city you chose.
   e. Click the Map link.
   f. Print the map and write your name at the top of the page. (You might need to click the Printable Map link near the bottom of the map to get a good copy.)

4. **Search periodical databases.**
   a. In the Online Companion, click the MagPortal link under "Periodical Listings."
   b. Search for a magazine article by typing your search terms in the Search text box.
   c. Scan the list of resulting articles and record one URL in the Skill #4 table in your document.
   d. In the Online Companion, click the FindArticles link under "Periodical Listings."
   e. Search for another article on the same topic.
   f. Scan the list of resulting articles at FindArticles and record one URL in the Skill #4 table in your document.
   g. Save and close the document, then exit your word-processing program.

5. Find government information.

 a. In the Online Companion, click the FirstGov link under "Government resources."

 b. Click the Advanced Search link, type senator in the all of these words text box, click the Search in list box, scroll down, then click Washington.

 c. Click Search.

 d. Find a Web page with a state senator's name on it.

 e. Print the Web page and write your name at the top of the page.

6. Find online reference sources.

 a. In the Online Companion, click the ipl Reference page under "Online References."

 b. Click the Style & Writing Guides link.

 c. Scroll down the page and click the Citing Electronic Resources link.

 d. Find a Web site that can help you cite documents in the APA style.

 e. Click the page name, print a copy, then write your name at the top of the page.

7. Find mailing lists and newsgroups.

 a. In the Online Companion, click the Google link under "Search Engines."

 b. Click the Groups tab above the Google Search text box.

 c. Click a type of group of interest to you.

 d. Choose a subgroup, browse the newsgroups, then click one.

 e. Find a thread of interest to you, then click that thread.

 f. Print the resulting archived message, then write your name at the top of the page.

8. Search with an intelligent agent.

 a. In the Online Companion, click the IncyWincy link under "Intelligent search agents."

 b. Click the Preference boost link, delete all the previously selected search Categories and associated Subcategories, select a new Category, click one or more Subcategories, then type a complex query.

 c. Click Search.

 d. Examine several of the search results.

 e. Print the first page of your search results, then write your name at the top of the page.

▼ INDEPENDENT CHALLENGE 1

You and a business associate are driving from London to York to visit some clients. As you haven't driven there before, you want to get driving directions.

    a. Go to the Online Companion at www.course.com/illustrated/research3, then click the MapQuest UK link (under "Other Resources").

    b. Find the section for driving directions.

    c. Enter the appropriate to and from locations and get the directions.

    d. On the resulting directions page, locate the Printer Friendly link, then click the link.

    e. Print a copy of the directions, then write your name at the top of the page.

Advanced Challenge Exercise

- While looking for maps, you decide to check the driving distance across Canada.
- Return to the Online Companion, click the MapQuest USA link, then click the Driving Directions icon. Note the driving distance between Quebec, QC, and Vancouver, BC.
- You realize the mileage quoted is while traveling much of the way in the United States. Because you particularly want the drive to remain in Canada, restate your query in several shorter trips to keep the directions within Canada. (*Hint*: If you want, you can use Quebec, QC, to Sudbury, ON, then Sudbury to Winnipeg, MB, then Winnipeg to Vancouver, BC.)
- Print a copy of your final driving directions, then write the total trip mileage and your name at the top of the page.

▼ INDEPENDENT CHALLENGE 2

You are flying to Sydney, NSW, Australia, on business. You are with a firm that specializes in designing Web sites for banks. Your company is going to design the Web site for the Waratah Mortgage Corporation, and you decide to check the Web for other banks you might visit while in Sydney. You look up phone numbers and locations of banks on your laptop.

    a. Go to the Online Companion at www.course.com/illustrated/research3, then click the Australian yellow pages link under "Yellow pages."

    b. From the information you know, set up an appropriate search.

    c. Find two banks that are located in Sydney.

    d. Print a map showing their locations, then write your name at the top of the page.

▼ INDEPENDENT CHALLENGE 3

You are thinking of immigrating to Canada and starting a business. You have heard there is a special business class immigration available.

    a. Go to the Online Companion at www.course.com/illustrated/research3, then click the Canadian Government Info link under "Government references."

    b. Locate an official Canadian government Web page that has the information you need.

    c. Print the page, then write your name at the top of the page.

▼ INDEPENDENT CHALLENGE 4

You want to learn more about the content hidden in databases on the Internet. Because news articles about the deep Web are likely to be stored in magazine archives (databases), you decide to use the intelligent search agent IncyWincy to search both the invisible Web and the visible Web.

a. Go to the Online Companion at www.course.com/illustrated/research3, then click the IncyWincy link under "intelligent search agents."

b. Use the Preferences link or Preference boost option to display a list of search Categories.

c. Scroll down the Categories list, click Computers, click the Internet check box, then click other Subcategories you think might contain information about the deep Web (for example, Computer Science, News and Media, and so on).

d. In the Search text box, type *"invisible Web" OR "deep Web"*, then click Search.

e. Scroll down and examine the results, then click Next to view the next 10 search results. Use the Previous link and Next link at the bottom and top of each page to move back and forth through your search results. Explore several pages to locate useful information.

f. Use your browser to print a page, then write your name and the title Invisible Web at the top of the printout.

g. Exit your browser.

Advanced Challenge Exercise

- You want to use a different intelligent search agent to see if it might find additional information about the invisible Web.
- Go to the Online Companion, then click the Turbo 10 link under "Intelligent search agents."
- In the Find databases relevant to text box, type *"invisible Web" OR "deep Web"*, then select the As a Boolean query option in the adjacent list box. Click Go.
- Print the results page, then write your name at the top of the page.
- Compare the first 10 search results from Turbo 10 with those from IncyWincy that you gathered in Steps a–g. How do the listings differ? From your research, does it appear useful to search more than one intelligent search engine?

▼ VISUAL WORKSHOP

Now that you know how to search the invisible Web, you want to use an intelligent search agent to check which sites you can turn up on one of your favorite hockey players. Go the the appropriate Web site and perform a search to locate the page shown in Figure D-19 (*Hint*: The site is listed in the Online Companion). Print a copy of the page, then write your name at the top of the page.

FIGURE D-19

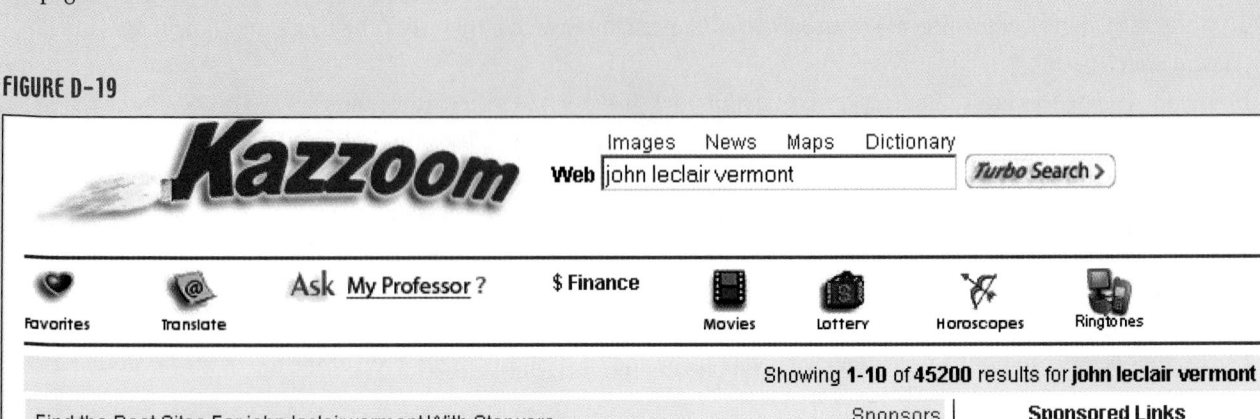

Showing **1-10** of **45200** results for **john leclair vermont**

Find the Best Sites For john leclair vermont With Starware
Starware search is an excellent resource for quali...
URL: search.starware.com

Sponsors

Sponsored Links

Looking For john leclair vermont
Find john leclair vermont and more at Lycos Search. No clutter, just answers. Lycos - Go Get It!
search.lycos.com

Pittsburgh Penguins - Team | Players
... Jan 16, 7:30 PM. John LeClair - #10. Position. Left Wing ... Born. St. Albans, Vermont / 07-05-69 ...
www.pittsburghpenguins.com

John LeClair - Pittsburgh Penguins - NHL - Yahoo! Sports
The latest stats, facts, news and notes on John LeClair of the Pittsburgh Penguins ... Fleury Sergei Gonchar Ric Jackman Konstantin Koltsov John LeClair Ryan Malone Josef Melichar Matt Murley Lyle ... Jul 5, 1969 - St. Albans, Vermont. Draft: 1987 - 2nd round (33rd overall ...
sports.yahoo.com

John LeClair NHL Hockey at CBS SportsLine.com
John LeClair NHL Hockey player profile pages at CBS SportsLine.com. ... 10 John LeClair, LW. Height/Weight: 6-3/228 ... Albans, VT, USA. Team: Pittsburgh. College: Vermont. NHL Experience: 14 ...
www.sportsline.com

Capital News 9 | 24 Hour Local News | SPORTS | Pens get Vermont native John LeClair
The Pittsburgh Penguins have added veteran John LeClair to their roster. LeClair, a Vermont native, has spent the last 10 seasons with the Flyers. ... Pens get Vermont native John LeClair. 8/16/2005 3:35 PM ... The Pens have signed high-scoring forward John LeClair, who was ...
www.capitalnews9.com

Pittsburgh Penguins - Team | Press Release: PENGUINS SIGN FREE AGENT LEFT WING JOHN LECLAIR
Jan 16, 7:30 PM. PENGUINS SIGN FREE AGENT LEFT WING JOHN LECLAIR. 08/15/2005. (Five-time League All-Star approaching 400 career goals coming to Penguins) ... The 6-3, 226-pound native of St. Albans, Vermont has appeared in at least 75 games in seven ...
www.pittsburghpenguins.com

UVM's John LeClair
University of Vermont Department of Classics: Athletics: John LeClair ... Cause Mr. LeClair got his 50th and he was one ... around the league, that John is one of the best ... all of us in Vermont, well we just think that ...
www.uvm.edu

John LeClair - Pittsburgh Penguins - Game Log - NHL - Yahoo! Sports
Current and comprehensive game log data for John LeClair ... Fleury Sergei Gonchar Ric Jackman Konstantin Koltsov John LeClair Ryan Malone Josef Melichar Matt Murley Lyle ... Jul 5, 1969 - St. Albans, Vermont. Draft: 1987 - 2nd round (33rd overall ...

Data Files List

Read the following information carefully!

It is very important to organize and keep track of the files you need for this book.

1. **Find out from your instructor the location of the Data Files you need and the location where you will store your files.**

   - To complete many of the lessons in this book, you need to use Data Files. Your instructor will either provide you with a copy of the Data Files or ask you to make your own copy.

   - If you need to make a copy of the Data Files, you will need to copy a set of files from a file server, standalone computer, or the Web to the drive and location where you will be storing your Data Files.

   - Your instructor will tell you which computer, drive, and folders contain the files you need, and where you will store your files.

   - You can also download the files by going to www.course.com. See the inside back cover of the book for instructions to download your files.

2. **Copy and organize your Data Files.**

   - Use the Data Files List to organize your files either on a Zip drive, network folder, hard drive, or other storage device.

   - Create a subfolder for each unit in the location where you are storing your files, and name it according to the unit title (for example, Internet Research Unit A).

   - For each unit you are assigned, copy the files listed in the **Data File Supplied column** into that unit's folder.

   - Store the files you modify or create in each unit in the unit folder.

3. **Find and keep track of your Data Files and completed files.**

   - Use the **Data File Supplied column** to make sure you have the files you need before starting the unit or exercise indicated in the **Unit and Location column**.

   - Use the **Student Saves File As column** to find out the filename you use when saving your changes to a Data File provided. (This information is also provided in the lesson, when you save each file.)

   - Use the **Student Creates File column** to find out the filename you use when saving your new file for the exercise.

Data Files List

Unit & Location	Data File Supplied	Student Saves File As	Student Creates File
UNIT A			
Lessons	IR A-1.doc	Searching the Internet	na
SR	IR A-2.doc	Internet Searches	na
IC1	na	na	Harrison
			Harrison ACE
IC2	na	na	UK Computing
IC3	na	na	My Topic
			My Topic ACE
IC4	na	na	Two Search Engines
VW	na	na	Hockey
UNIT B			
Lessons	IR B-1.doc	Complex Searches	na
SR	IR-B-2.doc	Boolean Searches	na
IC1	na	na	na
IC2	na	na	na
IC3	na	na	Library of Congress
IC4	na	na	na
VW	na	na	na
UNIT C			
Lessons	IR C-1.doc	Subject Guides	na
SR	IR C-2.doc	Using Subject Guides	na
IC1	na	na	WWII Posters
			WWII Posters ACE
IC2	na	na	RSS
IC3	na	na	Web site evaluation
IC4	na	na	My subject guide
			My subject guide ACE
VW	na	na	Hockey database
UNIT D			
Lessons	IR D-1.doc	Specialty Information	na
SR	IR D-2.doc	Specialty Searches	na
IC1	na	na	na
IC2	na	na	na
IC3	na	na	na
IC4	na	na	na
VW	na	na	na

Glossary

Algorithm A mathematical formula used by a search engine to rank each Web site returned in search results according to the terms used in the search query.

AND Boolean operator that connects keywords in a search query. AND narrows a search and decreases the number of search results because each keyword connected with AND must be on a Web page for it to be included in the results. Every additional keyword connected to a search by AND further narrows the search. *Note:* Most search tools use AND as the default Boolean operator, so entering it in your search query usually is unnecessary. If you're unsure how a search tool uses AND or the plus sign (+), read the tool's Help pages. *See also* Boolean operator.

AND NOT Boolean operator that connects keywords in a search query. Using AND NOT narrows a search and decreases the number of search results because each word must not be on a Web page for it to be included in the results. Every additional keyword connected to a search by AND NOT further narrows the search. *Note:* Most search tools require the use of the minus sign (-) to indicate AND NOT. If unsure how a search tool uses AND NOT or the minus sign (-), read the tool's Help pages. *See also* Boolean operator.

Annotation Summary or review of a Web page, usually written by experts, such as professionals, academics in the field, or librarians.

Bookmarks A function of the Netscape browser that allows for easy storage, organization, and revisiting of Web pages. This browser feature is called Favorites in Internet Explorer.

Boolean logic A logic system, based on simple algebra and developed by mathematician George Boole, which defines how Boolean operators manipulate sets of data. Also known as Boolean algebra. It is represented graphically with Venn diagrams.

Boolean operators Command words such as AND, OR, and AND NOT that narrow, expand, or restrict a search based on Boolean logic.

Cached page Copy of a Web page that resides on a search engine's computer.

Citation format A style guide that standardizes references to resources like books, magazine articles, and Web pages. Common formats are those by MLA (Modern Language Association) and APA (American Psychological Association).

Complex query A search query that uses Boolean operators to define the relationships between keywords and phrases in a way that search tools can interpret.

Corporate author A committee, association, or group credited with creating a work such as a Web page.

Deep Web *See* Invisible Web.

Default operator The Boolean operator that a search engine automatically uses in a query, whether typed as part of the query or not. Most search engines default to the AND operator, although a few default to the OR operator.

Dewey Decimal system A numeric subject classification system used in many libraries. Named after its inventor Melville Dewey.

Discussion group *See* Newsgroup.

Directory *See* Subject guide.

Distributed subject guide Subject guide created by a variety of editors working somewhat independently and usually stored on numerous computers around the country or the world. Like a regular subject guide, it hierarchically arranges links to Web pages based on topics and sub-topics. Though many distributed subject guides are excellent, they often lack standardization and can be uneven in quality. *See also* Subject guide.

Domain The last two or three letters of a URL. URLs from the U.S. typically end in three letters, indicating the type of site, such as *.gov*, *.edu*, *.org*, or *.com*. URLs from other countries typically end in two letters, indicating the country of origin, such as *.ca* (*Canada*), *.uk* (*United Kingdom*), or *.jp* (*Japan*).

Drilling down Clicking through subject headings (or topics or categories) to reach relevant links. Typically the subject topics are arranged from the more general to the more specific.

Dynamically generated Web pages Pages generated by a database in response to a specific query. One kind of page found in the invisible Web.

Evaluative criteria Standards used to determine if a Web site is appropriate for your needs. These standards usually include considerations of organization, authority, objectivity, accuracy, scope, and currency.

Favorites A function of the Internet Explorer browser that allows for easy storage, organization, and revisiting of Web pages. This browser feature is called Bookmarks in Netscape.

Filter *See* Search filter.

Forcing the order of operation Using parentheses in a complex query to force the search tool to look at the words inside the parentheses first, which can greatly affect search results. If not forced, search tools typically search keywords from left to right.

Forum *See* Newsgroup.

Hierarchy A ranked order. Hierarchies commonly used in Internet subject guides include topical, alphabetical, and geographical. Topical hierarchies typically go from the more general to the more specific.

HTML (Hypertext markup language) A coded format language used to create and control the appearance of documents on the Web. *See also* Web page.

Intelligent search agent A software program that automatically retrieves information stored on multiple databases and aids in accessing information on the invisible Web. Also called a search bot. Examples include ProFusion and IncyWincy.

Internet A vast global network of interconnected networks that allows you to find and connect to information on the Web.

Internet search tools Services which help locate information on the Web and the Internet, including search engines, metasearch engines, subject guides, specialized search tools, and intelligent search agents.

Intersection The place where two sets overlap in a Venn diagram. Results from the use of the Boolean AND.

Invisible Web The part of the Web inaccessible to search engine spiders. It consists of information housed in databases, as well as much of the Web's data in .pdf, .doc, and other non-HTML file formats. Also known as the deep Web. The invisible Web is many times, perhaps 500 times, larger than the visible Web. A small part of the invisible Web can be accessed with intelligent search agents.

Keyword An important word that describes a major concept of your search topic.

List address The mailing list address to which correspondence is sent. *See* also Subscription address.

Listserv A software program that supports interactive Internet communication, such as the use of mailing lists.

Mailing list A form of interactive Internet communication which allows e-mailing messages to all other members of a list automatically. Often called a Listserv after the software that supports it.

Metasearch engine A search tool that searches the indexes of multiple search engines simultaneously. Better metasearch engines, such as Ixquick and ProFusion, present your query to various search engines in the ways they will understand it. Since most do not, it is usually best to metasearch with only simple searches.

Minus sign Used by many search tools as a symbol for the Boolean AND NOT.

Mnemonic Assisting or aiding memory. For example, many URLs are mnemonic to make them easier to remember.

Netiquette The protocol and common rules of courtesy used by people on the Internet, particularly in discussion groups or newsgroups.

Newsgroup A form of interactive Internet communication which serves as a virtual bulletin board where messages on thousands of topics are posted daily. Often called a Usenet group after the software upon which it runs. Also called discussion groups and forums.

OR Boolean operator that connects keywords in a search query. Using OR broadens or expands a search and increases the number of search results because any of the words can be on a Web page for it to be included in the results. Every additional keyword connected to a search by OR further broadens the search. *See also* Boolean operator.

Order of operation *See* Forcing the order of operation.

Parentheses Used around two or more keywords combined with Boolean operators, parentheses force the order of operation of a search query by indicating that the part of the search inside the parentheses should be performed first.

Periodical database A specialized database that contains the full text of articles from periodicals, such as newspapers, magazines, and journals. Common periodical databases are ProQuest, InfoTrac, and EbscoHost. This kind of database usually requires a paid subscription and is only available at libraries.

Phrase searching Forcing the search tool to search only for pages containing a phrase, or two or more words together in a certain order. Typically quotation marks are used around the words to indicate that they should be searched as a phrase. Phrases can be used with Boolean operators in the same ways a keyword can be used.

Plus sign Used by many search tools to indicate the Boolean AND. Since AND is the default operator for most search tools, it is usually unnecessary to enter it in your search query. *See also* AND.

Portal A large Web gateway providing access to huge amounts of information. It often includes search engines, news, shopping, e-mail, chat, and more. A portal that focuses on one topic or industry is called a vertical portal or a vortal.

Query *See* Search query.

Quotation marks Used around two or more keywords in a search form, quotation marks indicate to most search tools that the words should be searched as a phrase.

Scope The range of topics covered by a Web site. The scope of a site may be narrow, covering a smaller range of topics, or broad, covering a wider range of topics.

Search bot *See* Intelligent search agent.

Search engine A search tool, usually indexed by spiders, that locates Web pages containing the keywords entered in a search form.

Search filter A program used by search tools, usually from Advanced Search pages, to specifically include or exclude Web pages according to criteria such as language, file format, date, and domain. Whenever a filter is used, results are limited. Every additional filter used in a search further limits the results.

Search form The place where a user enters a search query at a search tool. It can be one text box or a complex array of text boxes, filters, and drop-down menus.

Search query Keywords, phrases, and/or Boolean operators entered into a search form that the search tool uses to search its index.

Set The term used for a group in Boolean logic. In a Venn diagram a set is commonly represented as a circle.

Site map An index to the pages on a Web site.

Specialized search tool A Web site that provides access to data stored in online databases that require direct access, making traditional search engines and most subject guides ineffective. Specialized search tools include online telephone directories, reference tools, online maps, and online periodicals.

Specialized search engine A search engine that limits the Web pages it indexes by subject. A specialized search engine often combines the power of Boolean searching with the focus of a subject guide.

Spider A computer program that scans, or crawls, the Web to index Web pages. The spider-created index is searched when you query a search engine. Spiders do not make judgments regarding the value of indexing a page as human indexers do.

Stop words Common words, such as *a, and, the, for,* and *of* that are not normally searched by search tools.

Subject directory *See* Subject guide.

Subject guide A search tool that hierarchically arranges links to Web pages. The links are evaluated and annotated by people, usually subject specialists or librarians, as opposed to spiders. Also called subject directory, subject index, or subject tree.

Subject index *See* Subject guide.

Subject tree *See* Subject guide.

Subscription Payment made to the owner or distributor of digital information for online access for a specified period of time, usually a year.

Subscription address A mailing list address to which messages requesting e–mail addresses be added or dropped from a list are sent. Also known as the administrative address. *See also* List address.

Surface Web *See* Visible Web.

Synonyms Words that have similar meanings. In an online search, synonyms are normally used to expand a search. They are usually connected by the Boolean operator OR.

Syntax Rules of a language, like grammar, that standardize usage. In computer searching, syntax governs the form queries must take to instruct a search tool to perform a certain function.

T

hread A sub-topic of newsgroup postings. A discussion starts with one posting. Subsequent postings in response to it, no matter how many there are, are considered one thread.

Trailblazer page A Web page that links to numerous sites covering all aspects of a topic. Often trailblazer pages are compiled by experts in a field.

U

nion The combination of two sets in a Venn diagram. Results from use of the Boolean OR.

Usenet *See* Newsgroup.

V

enn diagrams Drawings, typically comprised of interacting circles, used to illustrate Boolean logic or searches using Boolean operators. First developed by mathematician John Venn.

Visible Web The portion of the Web that is indexed by search engine spiders. Also may refer to parts of the Web that, while not crawled by spiders, are indexed by subject guides. The visible Web, also known as the surface Web, is hundreds of times smaller than the invisible or deep Web.

Vortal A vertical portal. *See also* Portal.

W

eb *See* World Wide Web.

Web page The most common type of document on the World Wide Web. Most results from search engines and subject guides are Web pages, which are usually written in hypertext markup language, or HTML, and have file extensions of .htm or .html. Other types of file formats include .pdf (Adobe Acrobat), .ppt (PowerPoint), .xls (Excel), and .doc (WORD). These non-HTML documents are more likely to be part of the invisible Web and best accessed with intelligent search agents.

Web site Stores, links, and delivers Web pages. A Web site can range in size from one Web page to thousands of Web pages.

World Wide Web An enormous repository of information stored on millions of computers all over the world.

Index

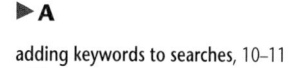